D1026934

In the Secret of His Presence

Helps for the Inner Life When Alone with God

By George Halley Knight

Published by Pantianos Classics

ISBN-13: 978-1-78987-031-2

First published in 1905

Contents

Preface

APART from strictly devotional books, a large proportion of the practical Christian literature of the day concerns itself rather with the outer manifestations of the Christian life than with its inner experiences. The Christian as he moves among men is in view, rather than the Christian as he is alone with God.

Books of this class are invaluable helps to Christian living, and can hardly be multiplied too much.

But, along with these, there may be some room for books of another class, books dealing specially with the inner soul-experiences which vitalise the life that is seen.

This volume is meant to be of such a kind to set forth in some degree the sacred privilege of secret fellowship with God, and to urge the need of making that intercourse with Him more frequent and more prolonged.

If it helps any reader of it to realise more fully the joy to be found in the secret place of meditation and prayer, its purpose will be fulfilled.

Garelochhead,
1905.

"By all means use some time to be alone;
Salute thyself, see what thy soul doth wear."

- George Herbert.

"When first thine eyes unveil, give thy soul leave
To do the like: our bodies but fore-run
The spirit's duty. True hearts spread and heave
Unto their God, as flowers do to the sun.
   Give Him thy first thoughts then, so shalt thou keep
   Him company all day, and in Him sleep."

- Henry Vaughan.

"Be still, my soul, be still!
   Something that ear hath never heard.
   Something unknown to any song of bird,
   Something unborne by wind, or wave, or star
   A message from the Fatherland afar
Comes to thee, if thou art but still."

- Anon.

I - The Need of Being Much Alone with God

HAS secret communion with God come to be one of the lost arts of the Church? Can it be the case, as it is often said to be, that comparatively few who name the Christian name, spend more than five minutes of each day alone with God? If so, the weakness, and worldliness, and unfruitfulness of the professing Church are explained at once. Our forefathers knew far more than we do of prolonged communion with God in the secret place; and there was a depth in their religion gained thereby which is greatly lacking now. No doubt their spiritual life was in some sense narrower than ours. It was more self-centred than was good for them. But with the widening of the stream, there has come a shallowing of it too; and if there is one call more imperative than another for every Christian ear to hear, it is the call " back to prayer: not less work, but more communion; not less activity in Christian effort, but more secret fellowship with God."

We live in a busy age. Life goes on at high pressure. From early morning till late evening the bewildering whirl of the world's machinery never stops. Both body and brain are exposed to incessant wear and tear. The necessary business of life seems to claim larger time than ever; and the passion for amusement which is so characteristic of the age comes in to seize upon whatever time is left by graver things; so that, between business on the one side and amusement on the other, leisure for prayer is well-nigh crushed out. That is an atmosphere in which no Christian can possibly thrive.

But even really earnest men, men who are not living for the world or for themselves, but for God, men whose energies are consecrated whose days are spent in sacred devotion to Christ, who find their joy in serving Him by serving men — even they need many a quiet hour alone with God if their power for service is to be maintained. When Luther was in the heat of his great conflict with Rome, and hour after hour was filled with the laborious work of preaching, writing, and disputing for the truth, he said, " I cannot get on without three hours of prayer every day." Even for the more secular work that lies to the hand of most of us, much prayer is needed if our wisdom and our strength for that work are not to fail. That noble Christian soldier, Have-lock, when overwhelmed with the strenuous labours that had to be gone through during the terrible months of the Indian Mutiny, so felt the absolute need of much secret prayer that he made it his rule when he had to march at eight to rise at six, and when he had to march at six to rise at four, in order to ensure for himself at least one morning hour of undisturbed communion with God before the pressure of the day's duties began. The same thing was seen in Livingstone when pioneering for Christ in Central Africa. His private journals show how very near to God he lived, and how his strength was gained by dwelling much in "the secret place of the Most High."

It was a distorted apprehension of this great truth that led so many in former days to retire from the world altogether, and live as hermits in the seclusion of mountain caves. It was not always to escape the persecutor's sword, neither was it always to' get away from the horrible corruptions of society into a purer moral atmosphere. It was often just to have more undistracted fellowship with God and larger leisure for meditation upon things divine. The method was a mistaken one and seldom served its end, but the aim was good.

The whole tendency of modern days, however, is to go to the opposite extreme, and make religion almost entirely a social thing. The dominant note of the Christian life amongst ourselves is the social one. The great difficulty in earlier times used to be to get men to be earnest enough to go *into* the world and sanctify *it.* Now the difficulty is to get them to be earnest enough to go *away* from the world and sanctify *themselves.* The religious life is identified with public gatherings, united worship, and an incessant round of activities in social Christian work; and it tends, on that very account, to be greatly unfamiliar with secret prayer, and private fellowship with God. There is unquestionably a danger in this, for ceaseless activity for others may weaken the spiritual life within ourselves, and force from us ere long the sad confession, "I have kept the vineyards of others, but mine own vineyard I have not kept." For stirring great enthusiasms we need the inspiration of the crowd; Christ's Gospel has always won its noblest triumphs in social revivals: but for the deepening and confirming of holy principles within us we need the seclusion of the "secret place." The trees in a forest grow tall but thin. They shoot up quickly through mutual support; but take away from any of them the shelter of its neighbouring trees, and, at the first blast of a hurricane it will fall. It is not there, but on some bare hillside where it has long battled with every wind that you must look for the tree that no storm can dislodge, that will outlast the shock of a hundred winter gales.

It can be no otherwise with ourselves. We may be *planted* in the kingdom with a multitude, but only in secret, lonely, personal fellowship with God can we really *grow* into the strength of "trees of righteousness" for Him.

What we need above all things in these crowded days is the setting apart of many *listening* times; times of quiet in which we can hear the heavenly voices that call to us unregarded in the busy day. The great clock bell of St. Paul's is not heard even a few streets off in the roar of traffic all day long; but it can be heard over half the metropolis in the silence of the night. One reason why God so often spoke to His servants in the night was that all was quiet then. That, too, was one reason why so many of them were sent away into desert solitudes that they might hear what He had to say. It may be one reason why sickness and sorrow are sent so frequently into our careless lives. God has something to say to us which, in the whirl of our earthly ambitions, we cannot hear: and He makes the noises of the outer world to cease that He may speak to the soul. Sometimes He "*tries us* in the night," sometimes He "*giveth songs* in the night," sometimes He "*instructs* us in the night," sometimes He gives us "*a vision* in the night ": but all of these we will utterly miss if there is no quiet time in which He can come very near to us, and we can come very near to Him. There are many ways of preparing to receive blessing from on high; but one of the most essential is this, "Commune with your own heart, and be still."

> "Serve God before the world: let Him not go
>   Until thou hast a blessing; then resign
> The whole unto Him, and remember who
>   Prevailed by wrestling ere the sun did shine.
> Rise to prevent the day. Sleep doth sins glut,
> And heaven's door opens when the world's is shut."

>   **- Henry Vaughan.**

> "Sum up at night what thou hast done by day;
> Dress and undress thy soul, mark the decay
> And growth of it: if, with thy watch, that too
> Be down, then wind up both. Since we shall be
> Most surely judged, make thy accounts agree."

>   **- George Herbert.**

II - All Doors That Open Earthward Must Be Shut When We Are Alone with God

"THE doors being shut." There is more in this simple phrase than meets the eye. It tells how the Risen One suddenly stood in the midst of His disciples in the fast-closed upper room on the evening of the Resurrection day, and, in so far, it is the record of a miracle. But it also contains a fine suggestion of a great spiritual truth; and it is noteworthy that it is to John, the most spiritual of the Evangelists, that we are indebted for our knowledge of the fact. The other Evangelists say only that the disciples were gathered in an upper room; but John adds the significant remark that "the doors were shut for fear of the Jews." They were not merely a secluded but a trembling company. Do what they could, try to believe as they might, they could not rise into the joy of the Resurrection. But the Risen One Himself came noiselessly and mysteriously into their midst with His words of peace. The same divine Lord who had come out of the grave in spite of the sealed stone, came into the upper room in spite of the closed doors, for no earthly barriers could hinder the perfect freedom of His glorified Resurrection life; and His greeting to them brought a gladness with it they had never known before.

But do not *all* His best visits to the soul take place only when, in a true, deep sense, the doors are shut? *We* need shut doors for our holiest intercourse with Him. *He* needs shut doors for His most comforting messages to us. The " still small voice " can be heard distinctly only when the noise of the world's voices is shut out, and we are as in a "secret place of the Most High." Was it not on this very account that the Lord, when giving a rule for prayer-intercourse with God, laid such emphasis on the seclusion and privacy of it? " Enter into thy chamber, and *when thou hast shut the door*, pray to thy Father who seeth in secret." " Let there be no ostentation in your praying," He says; but He means more than that, " let there be no hurry either, and no distrac-tion of soul; have a quiet place and a quiet time for prayer, but above all have a quiet heart."

No doubt there may be very sweet moments of prayer where there is no secret chamber with shut door, and no outward quiet either. Nehemiah could lift up his heart in prayer and get an immediate answer too, even while standing as cupbearer before the king, and carrying on a conversation with him all the time. So may the busiest of busy men in the very midst of their engrossing work, or when walking the crowded street — the tradesman amid the duties of shop or mill — hard-working mothers amid all the distrac-tions of their children's crics' — the traveller amid the noisy jolting of the railway train — all practise the art of sending glances and petitions upwards to the Throne on high, and know the comfort of getting immediate answers back that will make them calmer, wiser, braver than they were before. How strengthening such wayside prayers may be none know till they have prac-tised them. But if we are to know the *full* joy of intercourse with God, we must make definite room for it outside of the busy current of life, and set apart for it conscientiously some *quiet* time, even though that should need to be stolen from the morning slumber or the evening rest.

"Shut thy chamber-door," said Jesus when rebuking ostentation in prayer; and a literal obedience to that command may often be needed even yet: for the ostentation of the Pharisee who prayed at the corners of the street "to be seen of men " may be imitated to-day by those who pray in their own cham-bers, but leave open the chamber-door on the chance that some one may come in and find them on their knees, and think what good Christians they are — thus making a real parade of their devotion even while professing to conceal it! But the Lord's command goes farther than this. "Shut the door of thy heart" He says, for the heart-door may be left open to all the distractions and disturbances of earth, even though the room-door is closed. Many a Christian knows, from sad experience, that this is so. He is never so haunted by worldly cares and frivolous thoughts as when bending the knee in secret prayer. Not only the worries but the veriest vanities of life come crowding in just when he would seek to be alone with God. " Shut thy heart's door" there-fore, and *keep the world out*. A wind-tossed lake gives no reflection of the sky. We need to arrest all worldly things that would claim admission to the soul, and say to them as Abraham said to his servants at the foot of Mount Moriah, "Abide ye here while I go yonder to worship." " Shut the door of the heart," *and keep unbelief out.* Do not allow the secret misgiving that your prayers will not be of any use. God's answers are given only to a perfect trust. " Shut the door of thy heart," *and keep formality out.* Mechanical devotion does no man any good. To pray just to satisfy conscience because the set time for prayer has come and we must get through with the duty, is not only an attempt to impose upon God, it is practising a tremendous deceit upon ourselves. " Shut the door of thy heart," *and keep impenitence out,* for the heart may be really clinging to the very sin the lips are praying against. The only prayer that tells with God is the prayer that is absolutely guileless and sincere. "If I regard iniquity in my heart the Lord will not hear me." "Shut the door of thy heart," a*nd keep self-will out.* To ask God to ratify our own foregone determinations, or to fall in with our own desires, is not to pray but to *dictate* to Him. The undertone of every prayer must be, "not my will, but Thine be done." It may seem as if this must greatly limit the range of prayer, and even rob it of its charm as a practical help in life; but if we ask, and receive through asking, all it is His loving will to give, can we either wish or get a larger blessing than that?

There is thus to be a great shutting out, as well as a shutting in; but when the heart-door is firmly closed against all disturbances such as these, prayer-fellowship with the Lord will be one of our intensest joys: for the old experience of the Resurrection evening will be repeated again and again, " then came Jesus, *the doors being shut,* and said, Peace be unto you."

> "O Saviour! who, from earth's conflicting voices,
>   Art calling me to Thy seclusion sweet;
> Give me a heart that, still and calm, rejoices
>   To sit, with Mary, at Thy blessed feet.
>   For marvels of this secret place are known
>   To him who in it dwells with Thee, alone."

> — Tersteegen.

III - Christ Will Visit Us When We Prepare to Be Alone with Him

HE often comes to us unsought, and un-' — invited, surprising us with some word of peace when we are not expecting it. Even in the busiest moments of the day, in the throng and rush of troubling cares, He sometimes sends messages to the heart that are gladly recognised as His, and do much to sustain and cheer us. But is it not true of this Heavenly Friend, as it is true of many an earthly one, that He likes to be asked to visit us, and will sometimes wait for an invitation before He comes. If we want His presence with us, do we not need to prepare for receiving Him? Our hearts are often very Bethlehems; there is a great crowd, and " No room for Him in the inn ": and

10

He may sometimes, therefore, say in regard to His coming into the heart, "But withal prepare Me a lodging." The goodness which He has prepared for us He gives us only when He finds us preparing to receive it; and there is no place for that like the place of secret prayer.

But can any man really *expect* such visits from the Lord? Assuredly, if His own words are true, "If a man love Me ... I will love him, and will manifest Myself to him," "and My Father will love him, and we will come unto him and make our abode with him." On reading such words we might well be overwhelmed with surprise — the promise seems too great to be ever fulfilled! But very beautifully does the Lord lead up to His marvellous conclusion. First, He says, " I will love him ": but that might be only silent love, love really felt but unconfessed, and that would not satisfy us — nor does it satisfy Himself. For next. He says, "I will manifest Myself to Him." Still, even that might be only at a distance, or the medium of something else. So He adds, " We will come to him "; and even that is not all, " We will make our abode with him." That is not simply coming *near,* it is coming *in*; not only coming to visit, but coming to stay.

Now, do we ever think what it would be to have such a promise fulfilled to us in a literal and outward way; what it would mean to us if He should even for one day return to earth, and, in the same way as He used to frequent some earthly homes of old, should abide in ours? What would it be to have the Lord Jesus spending even one day beneath our roof, or talking to us even for one evening in the quiet family circle, consenting to be treated as our guest?

Does the thought ever occur to us, " What a home mine would be, if Christ were actually dwelling in it for a single week, going out and in, interesting Himself in all my concerns, sympathising both with my sorrows and with my joys, speaking to me of how I am living my life in the world here, directing me in all my difficulties, speaking to me, too, of things transcending this poor life altogether, telling me of the heavenly life for which He is preparing me, and bidding me be of good cheer! What an atmosphere of heaven would pervade that home of mine! What holy strength would come to me from that Divine companionship! What virtue would go out from Him to me! What peace His presence there would bring, and what holiness too! How heavenly-minded I would become! How radiant with a reflection of His sanctity! What a complete arrest His presence there would put upon every kind of sin! What a hushing there would be of all those tones of anger, irritation, selfishness, uncharitableness, that are so often heard from my lips! That home of mine would be, for the time, a miniature of heaven."

Do we ever think of all this? Then how wonderful the thought that something even better than all this would be is actually promised by Himself to all that " love Him "! and that better thing is to have Him in all the graciousness and power of His own glorious life, not merely an outward Visitant but an inward Resident, a Guest not merely in the home, but in the soul itself.

11

Did not Paul understand this well when he prayed for the Ephesians " that Christ might dwell in their hearts by faith"? This is much more than merely " thinking about Christ," more than '* imitating Christ," more than "following Christ," more than hanging up the portrait of Christ and looking at it. We hang some portrait of an absent one who is dear upon the wall of our room. Friends see it, and say, " What a speaking likeness that is! " We know what they mean, but we say to ourselves, " Alas! no, that is just what it cannot do — it cannot talk to me, it cannot advise me, it cannot comfort me: oh that these lips had language," but they are silent lips, the picture is a beautiful reminiscence, but that is all.

What Paul meant was not that we should just have our Christ in the Bible, like a portrait hung up before our eyes, but that we should have Christ in the heart, like a Friend whose living presence is in the home, a Friend accessible as counsellor and comforter every moment, a Friend to whom every doubt or sorrow or care can be freely opened out, and who will always speak to us His words of wisdom and of love.

"Master, where dwellest Thou?" said the first two disciples as they followed Jesus in the way. He answered them, " Gome and see." Now, He has no earthly home except His disciples' hearts; and yet there are some of these hearts that have Him so constantly within them that if the same question were asked Him to-day. He might take the questioner round to one after another of these disciples and say, "Come here and see."

Would that *all* disciples were such as these! How is it that we know so little of this blessed and intimate companionship with Christ? Simply because we so easily open the heart to all intruders, that " there is no room in the inn," and the Holy Christ goes away. Soon, perhaps, in penitence and shame we awake to our folly in thus banishing our Lord: we drive the intruders out, and cry to Him to return. He does return; but very speedily some fresh indignity put upon Him banishes Him again! And so the days go on, and the weeks too. He is never allowed thoroughly to occupy the place within us which we invite Him to fill; and His flying visits do not leave behind them any permanent fruit of holiness or of peace: He does not find the heart prepared for His coming, and does not get such a welcome as will induce Him to stay.

The leading idea of preparation for receiving a guest is anticipatory thoughtfulness, a consideration of what would please him when he comes. We fill his room with many small tokens of our wish that, in it, he should really feel at home. Do we ever so anticipate a visit from our Lord, and make the heart-room ready for Him before He comes? Do we ever feel as Moses felt when he said, "He is my God and I will prepare Him a habitation "? Perhaps we do: but even then we are confronted with two great obstacles — first, our conscious unworthiness to receive the Lord at all, and next, our felt incompetence so to purify the house that it shall be worthy to receive Him. We are therefore forced to take refuge in the paradox, that the Lord Himself must do in us what He asks us to do and what we are unable to do. We are to cleanse the heart for Christ to dwell in it, and yet it is just His own coming into it that alone can cleanse it thoroughly. If He comes to us at all He must come to us, unworthy of His presence as we are; and then what our own power cannot do. His power working in us will speedily do.

Our prayer must therefore be, " Lord, take my heart and cleanse it, for I cannot cleanse it myself; keep it Thyself, for I cannot keep it for Thee." And He will answer the prayer. He will bring these poor sinful hearts of ours into such close fellowship with Himself that His holy nature will be transfused into ours; moment by moment we shall become larger sharers in His victory and His peace: and the hearts in which He dwells will become living temples, full of " thanksgiving and the voice of melody."

"Sweet is the hour of secret prayer,
Sweet, with the hush of falling eve
To bend the knee with reverent air,
And words to the Unseen to weave.
How burns the fragrant incense poured
In quiet haunts at close of day
From loving hearts that, like their Lord,
Steal from the world to pause and pray!"

- **C. L. Ford.**

IV - The Great Divine Example of Being Much Alone with God

THERE had been a great festal gathering in Jerusalem. Multitudes had come to it from all parts of the land; and Jesus had come to it from Galilee. It was almost over. The Temple courts were emptying. The crowds that had been living for a week past in booths on the house-roofs were all dispersing to their homes, and the lonely Stranger whose voice had thrilled so many, and startled some, and angered others, had also to go away, for nowhere in all that city had a resting-place been provided for Him. "Every man went to his own home: Jesus went to the Mount of Olives."

How full of pathos these few simple words! We picture Him slowly, silently wending His way through the crowd as the evening shadows fall, and overhearing, as He goes, remarks passing from lip to lip about Him — some of them appreciative and kind, some indifferent, some contemptuous, and some full of hate. We see the crowd slowly thinning as street after street is passed; one door after another opening to receive the inmates of the various homes; we think of the companies reassembling within them for the evening meal and interchange of talk: and then we think of that lonely Stranger still passing on, no friendly door opened for *Him,* no voice of welcome inviting

Him — passing on and out by the city gate, and up the long slope of the olive-shaded hill to find *His* resting-place beneath the stars.

The homeless Man of Sorrows had no private prayer-chamber whose door He might shut to talk with God. No man offered Him a place where He might lay His head. Well, He would lay it down beneath His Father's trees, upon His Father's breast.

But this was no exceptional thing with Him. It was His habitual practice all along, even though some friendly home was willing to shelter Him. Again and again in the Gospel story we read such words as these: " He withdrew Himself into the wilderness and prayed "; "Rising up a great while before day, He departed into a solitary place, and there prayed "; and what strikes us with surprise is to find that frequently such a night of solitary prayer came in between two days each of which was so filled with labours of love for others that He had scarce one hour in them to call His own, and " no leisure so much as to eat."

Two very significant facts, when brought into connection with this, throw a wonderful light upon these secret hours of His.

One of these facts is that He was never for one moment of any day out of touch with God. We are constantly getting out of touch with God. The business and the cares of the world together come sadly in between us and God, and we need quiet seasons of retirement to bring us into touch with Him again. But Jesus always lived in the closest fellowship with the Father. He could speak of Himself as the "Son of Man who is in heaven." He was speaking and listening to the Father all day long, and yet He who was in such constant touch with God felt the need, as well as the joy, of more prolonged and more quiet communion with Him.

The other fact is, that most of the reasons that drive *us* to prayer could never have driven Him. He had no sins to confess, no mistakes to regret, no pardons to seek, no defeats in a struggle with inborn corruption to lament, no infirmities of temper to deplore, not even a momentary forgetfulness of His Father's will to repent of at His feet. Indeed, we owe our salvation to the fact that, living in our own nature, in the midst of our own temptations. He alone of men could pray without repentance, without the confession of a single sin, without either needing forgiveness or asking to be forgiven.

And yet He needed prayer. He loved it, but He needed it too; needed it, just as we need it ourselves, not only to refresh His soul after the disappointments of the day, but to nerve it for fresh labours sure to involve fresh pain on the day that was coming.

In a natural fear of lowering the Divine dignity of Christ we often forget His true humanity. We think of His earthly life as moving on a plane so different from ours that no parallel can be drawn between them. We find it difficult to think of Him as feeling in the various experiences of life anything like what we feel in the same; and if any striking instance of superiority in Him to our customary weaknesses presents itself, we account for it by referring it to

14

His Divine nature; and having accounted for it thus, we give up all idea of attempting to resemble Him. What we forget is that He too needed to walk by faith, needed to be filled with the Holy Spirit, needed to be lifted above natural discouragements, needed the sympathy of loving friends, needed the strengthening that is gained in private prayer. His strong and beautiful, serene and holy life so fills the eye, that we lose sight of His secret intercourse with the Father, out of which came all its beauty and all its power.

For they were no mere formal acts, these prayers of His. He was not just giving His countenance to a pious practice needed by us, but not needed by Himself. They were *real* prayers. If they were not so, if they did not spring out of a real feeling of need, if they were not prayers of dependence and of faith, they could be no examples to us. They would even have been misleading examples, teaching that the value of prayer consists merely in the length of time consumed by it. But He was *really* praying, and not apparently only, when alone with the Father. He prayed for others, but He prayed also for Himself; for He was not half human and half Divine, but wholly human though wholly Divine, compassed with all our human infirmities, and subject to our weaknesses as well; and therefore He needed prayer, needed it to strengthen Him, and needed it to keep Him calm.

Even to " the Lord of Glory " prayer was as the vital breath. He lived in the atmosphere of prayer from first to last; and when any specially important work had to be done, any specially difficult crisis had to be faced, any specially trying experience had to be endured, He met it by *special* prayer.

At His baptism He prayed. At the choosing of the twelve Apostles He prayed. Before doing many of His mighty works He prayed, and He prayed also after they were done. At His transfiguration He prayed. It came to Him in the very act of prayer. At the grave of Lazarus He prayed. When the popular enthusiasm was eager to make Him a worldly King He prayed. He prayed when the enthusiasm cooled, and rejection came. With prayer He entered on the day of His last sufferings. With prayer He agonised in dark Gethsemane. With prayer He cast His murderers upon the mercy He knew to be in the Father's heart. With prayer He looked up for support in the darkness of desertion on the Cross. In prayer He breathed out His Spirit into the Father's hands. If *He* needed prayer so constant, so filial, so dependent as this, how infinitely more do we!

There are mysteries in prayer that we cannot solve: but even though it were a greater mystery than it is, how the prayer of man can affect the heart and hand of God, how He who governs the universe by strict laws can interpose to help His children who are enveloped in these laws, we can face it calmly as we look upon the Man Christ Jesus pouring out His soul in "strong crying and tears." It answers a thousand difficulties just to see the Saviour on His knees — for *He* knew all the laws of the universe better than the wisest philosopher can do, and *He* would not have cried to God for help if it is impossible for God to answer such a cry. Jesus on His knees shows us that we are not helplessly enclosed in an iron network of natural laws preventing any succour in a time of need. Perplexities somehow vanish, and courageous hope comes in, the moment that we think of Him thus pleading trustfully with a Father who is in heaven. Perhaps, after all, the best answer to the question, "Why should I pray so much? " is this — " Because Jesus did." He who was "in all things made like unto His brethren" would have His brethren in all things made like to Him. As He was, so must we be in the world, and, characteristically, men of prayer. The praying Christian alone is the overcoming Christian, the holy Christian, the shining Christian, the Christian whose life is one long service of the Master, and whose heart is filled with the Master's joy.

"Master, where abidest Thou?
We would leave the past behind,
We would scale the mountain's brow,
Learning more Thy heavenly mind.
Canst Thou take our sins away?
May we find repose in Thee?
From Thy gracious lips to-day
As of old breathes ' Come and see.'"

- **The Three Wakings.**

"Allured up to the mountain-top, with God alone, apart,
There Spirit meeteth spu'it, there speaketh Heart to heart
There God and I — none other; His secret place I find
A home of isolation sweet, all trouble left behind."

- **Tersteegen,**

V - We Reach A Mountain-Top of Vision When Alone with God

THERE seems to be a rich suggestiveness in the fact that Jesus so often chose not merely a lonely but a lofty place for His fellowship with God. He seemed to love the *mountain* solitude as a place of prayer. Did He, the Great Lord, feel as we sometimes do, the mysterious power of altitude, as well as solitude, drawing Him nearer to heaven? He was " in all things made like unto His brethren " — was this one of them?

Some can remember times when strange and glad upliftings of soul were felt on the summit of a lofty hill, where they sat looking out with hushed soul upon God's majestic peaks, all glistening white with the purity of untrodden Alpine snow. They had moments of heavenly, as well as earthly, vision there; moments in which they felt so freed from the narrowing limitations of the ordinary world, and also from its baffling haze, that the soul seemed to leap

16

into larger freedom also, and they had clearer, serener, more entrancing views of God and of the things above than they ever enjoyed below.

Did ever Jesus feel this elevating and calming power of mountain solitude upon His perfectly human soul? We like to think He did. But, however that may be, His practice does suggest that what we need for our best fellowship with God is not solitude only, but height: that the prayer-chamber should be to us a place where we can look down upon our daily life as we would look from a mountain summit on the plain beneath; that there the noises of our daily business and anxieties should be hushed; and that there we should gain a larger outlook than is possible lower down.

It is nearly impossible for one who never gets above a level plain to understand his limitations, or to form a just estimate of his narrow life; but, looking down upon it from a height, he sees things in their right proportions; the apparently great are contrasted with the really great, the things close at hand are measured by the immensities beyond them. What he thought of as a great city becomes a mere speck in the distance; the mighty river is only a silver thread; the towering cathedral is so dwarfed as to be hardly visible; what he used to speak of as his encircling hills are shorn of the smallest pretension to the name. And then, too, as these apparent magnitudes dwindle into insignificance, larger and hitherto unsuspected magnitudes come into view.

Something like this is gained when, in a quiet hour of meditation and prayer, we are lifted above the world in which we ordinarily move. Many a false estimate is rectified there. Our ambitions, plans, labours, worries, vexations, sorrows, cares, fall into their true proportions. We can measure them and test them as we there look down upon them, till we come to see them just as they are seen by God Himself. We sometimes speak of getting from a mountaintop "a bird's-eye view" of things. From the mountain-top of secret prayer we get a "God's-eye view" of everything; and it is marvellous how that makes many great things look small, and small things great; how all mere worldly ambitions look surprisingly poor, and heavenly ambitions the only ones worth having. There is a wonderful reversal of estimates there; but to gain it is worth the climb; for, descending the hill, we can carry away with us the vision of the mountain-top to sanctify all our feelings when busy with things below.

It is only by going daily in this way above the world, and looking down upon it, that we can become really superior to its false attractions, and meet them with nobler ambitions stirring in the breast, and the light of heaven shining on the face.

Our Lord and Master's experience may help us here. It was while He was praying on a mountain-top that He was suddenly transfigured, and the glory of heaven so shone out in Him that the three disciples who "were with Him in the holy mount " were blinded by the lustre of it. Now the Lord did not go up that mountain in order to be transfigured. He went up to *pray.* The dark shadow of the coming Cross was over Him already, and the horror of it as

17

affecting His disciples made Him seek some comfort from the Father for *them* in prospect of it, as well as for Himself; and the glorious Transfiguration was God's answer to the prayer. And just as it was while praying that Jesus was *instantaneously* transfigured, so it is by prayer that His disciples are *gradually* transfigured till they also can shine with the reflected beauty of heaven.

That such an effect should be the outcome of long-continued faithful fellowship with God in secret will not seem wonderful if we consider what true prayer is. It is the direct contact of the soul with God. In this divine companionship we get completely out of contact with the things below, and stand face to face with Him near whom none can long be without catching something of His glory. All prolonged contact with earthly things tends to make us earthly in feeling and in life. All really close and prolonged contact with heaven must tend to make us heaven-like, and, therefore, God-like too.

The very countenance of a man of much prayer will often bear witness to his acquaintedness with the mountain-height. It will show a softened spiritual beauty that in his prayerless days it never had. But whether the face bears witness to the mountain-top or not, the whole life and character will. There is sure to be seen in his whole tone an elevation of feeling showing clearly that he is accustomed to be often very near to God: and thus his high fellowship with God will bring about a high life before men. If any Christian finds that his soul is not sufficiently raised above the down-dragging influence of earthly things, and his life not transformed, gradually but surely, into the beauty of holiness, it is only because he does not often enough climb the hill of secret communion with God, nor linger long enough there to catch its heavenly glow.

We need to be much in the company of God if we are to understand God, to sympathise with God, to feel as God feels, to resemble God. Two human hearts that are constantly together, dwelling in the same house, sharing the same table, talking with each other, finding each other's presence a daily joy, get in time wonderfully to resemble each other in all their habits of life, in their way of looking at life, in all their feelings about life, even in the very tones of the voice. It is this kind of intimacy with God that we need to cultivate; an intimacy that will enable us to understand God in all the ways of His Divine love, and will prevent us from misunderstanding Him when His love is a little concealed; an intimacy that will gradually make us resemble God too, lifting us into a region purer and loftier than other men know anything of.

> "When one that holds communion with the skies,
> Has filled his urn where these pure waters rise,
> And once more mingles with earth's meaner things;
> 'Tis even as if an angel shook his wings:
> Immortal fragrance fills the circuit wide,
> And tells us whence his treasures are supplied."

18

We must go upward as well as onward in our acquaintance with God, and linger long amid the glories of the mountain vision, if we are to come forth radiant from the secret place, and be shining witnesses to a shining Lord.

"Search me, God! my actions try,
    And let my life appear
As seen by Thine all-searching eye, —
    To mine my ways make clear.

Search all my thoughts, the secret springs,
    The motives that control;
The chambers where polluted things
    Hold empire o'er the soul.

Search till Thy fiery glance has cast
    Its holy light through all,
And I by grace am brought at last
    Before Thy face to fall."

Rev. F. Bottome.

VI - We Estimate Ourselves Aright Only When Alone with God

"BEFORE I can have any joy in being alone with God I must have learned not to fear being alone with myself. If my heart is not right with God I cannot possibly delight in fellowship with Him; and I cannot be right with Him until I am right with myself. My shrinking from close companionship with Him in the secret place may be due to the fact that I am *indifferent* to His presence, and do not care to speak to Him or to hear Him speak to me; but it may sometimes be due to another fact — that I am afraid of God, and therefore *afraid* to see myself as I appear to Him; afraid to give my conscience the chance of speaking to me more loudly than I like; afraid to look very narrowly into myself, lest I should make discoveries too destructive of my self-esteem, disconcerting me by tearing away every shred of that good opinion of myself in which I have been living contentedly for long; afraid, that is, to see myself as God sees me, and as I really am.

This shrinking from any deep self-scrutiny is by no means an uncommon thing, and often goes far to explain the feverish restlessness with which a world-loving heart plunges into a perpetual round of gaieties and dissipations. It is not always that any great satisfaction is found in these things, but they serve as an escape from troublesome questions about the soul, and help to get rid of the clamours of conscience that would be unbearable if any quiet hour were left in which its accusing voice might be listened to.

But something must be terribly wrong with any man who is afraid to be alone with himself. Humbling and saddening then made may be, but to face them honestly is the only way to life and peace. Every one who " comes home to God " must first, like the prodigal, " come to himself "; and there is no place like the chamber of quiet thought and prayer for that.

Job learned it there. It was when all other voices were hushed, and God's voice alone was heard, that he came to see his sinfulness and feel it so acutely that he cried, " Behold, O Lord, I am vile, and what shall I answer Thee? " Largely upright though he had been, a man of blameless life, "fearing God and eschewing evil," he had never before sounded the depths of his sinfulness. The unjust suspicions and accusations of his three friends only helped him to justify himself and blinded him to the real truth. But when face to face with God all illusions vanished, and he said, "I repent in dust and ashes."

It was when alone with God that *Isaiah* learned to feel in the same way. Sitting apart from all, he had a wonderful vision of the Seraphim in the Holy Place and heard the music of their praise; and then there flashed into him the thought of the contrast between himself and them, and he could only cry, " Woe is me! for I am undone; I am a man of unclean lips, for mine eyes have seen the King, the Lord of hosts." We might have expected to hear him say, "Blessed are mine eyes, for they have seen the King, the Lord of hosts," but we hear only an exclamation of intensest self-condemnation and shame. He saw the Seraphim bathed in the holiness they were singing of, and there flashed upon him the humbling thought of his own unlikeness to them. " How could I stand beside these holy ones? how could I sing in that heavenly choir, even though a golden harp were given me? Heaven so pure and my own heart so unclean, woe is me! I am farther off from God than I supposed myself to be! "

Isaiah was a true man of God, a sanctified man, a greatly sanctified man, perhaps the holiest man then living on the earth; and yet one glimpse of God in the secret place gave him such a glimpse of himself as made him fall down in deepest penitence and shame before the thrice-Holy One.

There is nothing like this coming face to face with God in secret for stripping off all the common conventional disguises of our sins and showing us the naked truth. When the light of heaven is there let into the dark corners of the soul, there come astonishing discoveries of sins that the darkness had concealed.

Sitting on a bright summer day among the stones half-hidden by the grass and heather of some warm hillside, admiring one of them gay with the colours of lichen and moss, and listening to the joyous song of some happy bird that has perched upon it, we seem to be looking on a perfect picture of purity and peace, till some sudden impulse makes us overturn the stone to see what is beneath. And then, what a revulsion of feeling! A whole colony of loathsome, wriggling creatures, disturbed by the light, are rushing hither and thither, burrowing out of sight into congenial darkness again! So will the light of God, when suddenly let in upon what lies beneath the fair exterior of life, reveal in one moment a multitude of sins that were never suspected to be there.

Not worldly men alone but even the best of Christians find this to be true. The saintliest are always the humblest. Growth in holiness can be measured by the acuteness of the consciousness of remaining sinfulness. The more our prayers for enlightenment are answered, the more our deep sinfulness comes into view. Was not this exemplified in the experience of that saintly man, the Apostle Paul? In the year 59, writing to the Corinthians, he calls himself *"the least of the Apostles."* Five years later, in the year 64, writing to the Ephesians, he calls himself *"less than the least of all saints ";* and in the year 65, when just finishing his course and ready to enter into his Master's joy, he writes to Timothy and calls himself *"the chief of sinners."* His sins seem to grow behind him as the love and glory of Christ grow before him. Christ's grace seems larger for his enlarging view of his sins, and his sins seem greater for his increasing sense of the love that has washed these sins away.

It cannot be safe for us to be blind to the sins which God sees clearly enough; and yet how greatly we ignore that large region of our sinfulness that is below the surface, out of the view of others, and often out of our own view too! Open sins we easily detect, and perhaps confess, but sins of thought and imagination and feeling — the deep stirrings of pride and vanity, of covetousness and impurity, of resentment and envy and discontent — we hardly think of these; or, if we do, we excuse them easily as being just sins of our nature and temperament and constitution, for which we are hardly responsible, or at least much less responsible than we are for open sins.

All self-deceptions such as these will perish when we are really alone with God. In the secret of His presence, and under its all-revealing light, we will see that our worst sins are not the open ones (great as these may be) that are only exceptional, but the hidden sins, continually active though working in the dark; just as an army of white ants will pick a carcase clean sooner than a lion will.

It is very significant that in Solomon's catalogue of " six things which the Lord hates, yea, seven which are an abomination unto Him," the very foremost place is given to what few men would consider a sin at all — " a proud look, a lying tongue, hands that shed innocent blood, a heart that deviseth wicked imaginations, feet that are swift to run to mischief, a false witness that speaketh lies, and he that soweth discord among brethren." A black catalogue that! most of them sins that all men will condemn, and of which most men would be ashamed. But at the very head of the list stands the "proud look," and as there cannot be a proud look unless there is a proud heart behind it, it is the hidden pride of heart that here is stamped with the foremost reprobation of God. When the sanctimoniousness of the Pharisee in the temple was scathingly held up to view by Jesus Christ, the working of his proud heart was unmistakably seen. His words, " God, I thank Thee that I am not as other men," were no expression of indebtedness to God. They meant simply, "I have great reason to congratulate myself." The mask of saintliness that gained him credit in the eyes of men was torn off by the only hand that could do it, and then the proud heart (the parent of the proud look) stood revealed. Therefore it is that when Christ speaks of the distinguishing marks of the heirs of His kingdom, He puts in the foreground that deep humility which is the direct opposite of the proud heart, and says, " Blessed are the poor in spirit, for theirs is the kingdom of heaven." So, too, when the disciples came asking Him, "Who is the greatest in the kingdom of heaven?" He took a child and set him in their midst and answered, " Whosoever shall humble himself as this little child."

The road of self -humbling is the only road that leads to peace and honour at last "Stoop! stoop!" said Samuel Rutherford writing to a most pious and godly friend — "Stoop! stoop! it is a low, low door by which we enter the kingdom of God." Nowhere can we learn this so well as in the secret place where we are alone with God.

"Thou knowest, Lord, the weariness and sorrow
Of the sad heart that comes to Thee for rest;
Cares of to-day, and burdens of to-morrow,
Blessings implored, and sins to be confessed.
I come before Thee, at Thy gracious word.
And lay them at Thy feet, — Thou knowest. Lord."

- Jane L. Borthwick.

VII - Our Perfect Freedom of Confession When Alone with God

IN the secret of His presence we can lay bare to Him, without fear, the inmost secrets of the soul. This is what we cannot do even to the dearest friend on earth. It is what we sometimes *dare* not do. Our lips are sealed for very shame. But freely and unrestrainedly we can confide our most secret shames and sadnesses to the ear of our listening Lord. It is this that makes the prayer-chamber a place of such infinite *relief* to an overburdened spirit.

There is a most suggestive argument in the Epistle to the Hebrews that makes God's perfect knowledge of us the very ground of our freedom in prayer. "All things are naked and opened unto the eyes of Him with whom we have to do." What then? "Let us, therefore, tremble before Him and shrink from His eye"? Not so: "Let us, therefore, come boldly to the Throne of Grace, that we may obtain mercy, and find grace to help in time of need." A surprising argument, but a very comforting one. It may look the very opposite of comforting to remind us of One whose knowledge of us is so minute: and so, when we go on to read of the sympathy of a tempted Christ, we might suppose that that consideration was brought in merely to neutralise the oppressiveness of the Omniscience. But the truth is that even Divine sympathy would be of very little use to us unless it were based upon a perfect knowledge of every element in the case: otherwise it would be an ignorant sympathy; and an ignorant sympathy can do no one much real good.

Is it not so even in human things? You are in trouble and perplexity because your worldly affairs have all gone wrong. Extrication from your difficulties seems impossible. You go to consult a wise friend about the case, and you lay before him a pretty full statement of it, but do not tell him *all.* Some of your transactions that look to yourself and will look to others decidedly dishonest you conceal, either from shame or fear. Your friend gives you the best advice he can: but it does not relieve you much. You cannot act upon it, because you see clearly that it is based upon a very imperfect knowledge of what the case really is. Finding you ere long still in the depths of gloom, he says to you, "I suspect you are keeping something back; you have not confided everything to me: if I am to be of real service to you, there must be no half-confidences, I must know the very worst; you must honestly tell me *all.*" And then you do tell him all. It costs you something to lay bare to him your hidden sins: but the next moment you are surprised to hear him say that now, for the first time, he sees the true way of relief. He can help you just because he knows the very worst about you. Is it not just in this way that God's perfect knowledge of us becomes an assurance to us that He can really help us in our time of need? What He says to us is, "*Because* I know everything about you, come with boldness to my Throne of Grace."

This is a surprising argument perhaps: but it will not be a wholly surprising one to those who know what the heart of God really is. Have we ever noted what kind of words the Bible uses to describe that heart? It speaks not only of the " grace " that is in it, but of the "*riches* of grace; and *exceeding* riches of grace"; not only of the "kindness" that is in it, but the "*loving* kindness "; not only of the "mercies" that are in it, but the "*tender* mercies." There is in us such a thing as kindness without love; there is sometimes love without kindness. But there is a sweet compound of both of these, making "lovingkindness," and that is found in perfection in the heart of God. There are in us mercies that are not particularly tender. It is a mercy often to a child to chastise it for its wilfulness; it may be a mercy to a criminal to shut him up in prison; but there is nothing very "tender" in either of these operations. There is a "tenderness," too, that is deficient in real mercy. It is mere weak, foolish, hurtful, goodnatured indulgence. But mercy and tenderness can also be combined; and for their perfect combination we must look into the heart of God. And it is there that the Apostle bids us look for our encouragement to " come boldly to the Throne of Grace."

What most of all prevents our coming boldly is our deep consciousness of sin. An overwhelming sense of sin makes us doubtful of a welcome if we should draw nigh. Prayer to the Infinitely Holy One, who is also the Infinitely Knowing One, seems almost an insult when uttered by creatures so unholy as we feel ourselves to be. But it is that Holy One Himself who says, " Put all that consciousness of My knowledge of your worst as an argument on the other side; precisely because I do know all, trust Me to be able to help you when you come." The argument is just: for, if He knows *all* about us, He knows more than merely our sins. He knows our difficulties, our infirmities, our struggles, our temptations, our conflicts, our longings, our aspirations; and His heart is going out to us in deep compassionating love, even when (judging Him by ourselves) we think of Him as standing sternly aloof from us, coldly and critically and accusingly looking on from a distance.

Surely there is nothing so little understood as the Heart of God, else we would never be afraid to go to Him with our sins, as well as with our griefs: for there is nothing in which He spends His blessed life more gladly than in pardoning and helping sinners. The largeness of His Heart does not wait till the worthiness of man can meet it. He deals with us in a way of transcendent generosity. His love is always far ahead of our prayers. He ^'prevents us with the blessings of goodness ": and, when any downcast heart cries out to Him in its sinfulness, quicker than a lightning flash His love leaps to the conclusion of mercy; and ere the broken prayer is half uttered, the mercy is on its way.

We thus see how the distrust that so often oppresses us at the very door of the secret place is to be overcome. It is by having the very largest conceptions of the heart of God in Jesus Christ. We make our sin an argument for fearing God. He makes it an argument for coming nigh. The utmost we can think of Him as saying is, "*Although* you are sinful, you may come." He puts it quite another way, "*Because* you are so sinful, come — come because you need Me so much." Alas for all of us, if we needed to stop sinning before we could confidently pray! Alas for us if only perfect men could come boldly to the Throne of Grace! If we go to God at all, we must, like the prodigal, go in our rags, and hunger, and sin, and utter need: but the compassionate Father, whose heart has never changed, will see us while we are yet " a great way off " — for He has been on the outlook for us, waiting for our coming — and He will shorten the distance between us and Him by going forth to meet us: and ere we have got half of our weeping confession out. He will be calling for the robe, and the ring, and the fatted calf, and giving us such a welcome as we never hoped to find.

"Thou knowest, not alone as God All-Knowing,
As man, our mortal weakness Thou hast proved
On Earth, with purest sympathies o'erflowing,
O Saviour! Thou hast wept, and Thou hast loved:
And love and sorrow still to Thee may come.
And find a hiding-place, a rest, a home."

- Jane L. Borthwick.

24

VIII - The Comfort of Christ's Sympathy Felt When Alone with God

IF it is an encouragement to us in the secret place of prayer that we have a Divine Listener who knows us thoroughly, it is a further encouragement that we have a Divine Sympathiser who can feel for us as well: "a Great High Priest who is passed into the heavens," who "knows what sore temptations are, for He has felt the same." The word "High Priest" has, to our modern ears, no very special or tender significance; but to an ancient Jew it was as significant as the word "Mother" is to us. The High Priest was the living embodiment of God's pity for the sinful: and he was "taken from among men" that he might be able to understand men when pleading for them with God. It will help us greatly, in the secret place, to think of Jesus as our High Priest, "made like His brethren" that His own experience of temptation might qualify Him for being a sympathising listener to their confessions at His feet.

It helps us greatly to think of Him as "in all points tempted like as we are." It is not said that He was tempted *in all circumstances* like ourselves. We find ourselves in circumstances where Christ never was: and we might, therefore, be inclined to say, " He was never situated just as I am, in business, or in society, or in domestic life; and however He may pity me. He cannot sympathise with me here." But He was tempted *in all points* as we are. There was no part of His human nature that temptation did not assail. Every sense and every faculty which in us is attacked by temptation, was attacked in Him. By sight, by sound, by touch, by taste, by love, by fear, by shame, by ambition, by doubt, by despair. He was assailed just as any of ourselves. In all points, on all sides of His nature, He was tempted like us, though not by the same things: and so He can understand and sympathise with us as none else can do.

It helps us, too, to think of Him as one who "suffered being tempted": for if it was in some way pain to Him to resist and overcome, He can sympathise with the pain temptation brings on us. The pain of it in His case was due to the fact that He was so perfectly human as well as perfectly Divine, and His human nature, like our own, had sensibilities easily wounded and weaknesses easily played upon. When tempted in the wilderness, it was His bodily hunger and the weakness caused by it that made the temptation sore. He might have overcome without any pain if the temptation had come immediately after that wonderful scene when, at His baptism, the Holy Ghost descended on Him, and He heard the voice from heaven, "This is My beloved Son": for when the soul is at the white heat of a great enthusiasm, glowing with the fire of the Spirit, any assault scarcely touch it. In a high spiritual temperature, we are almost above some forms of temptation. Evil suggestions die as soon as they are born. They fall like arrows on a shield of triple brass. But the tempter waited till the bodily exhaustion of Jesus gave him a chance he never had before: and it is from our weakness, too, that temptation borrows all its force. A temptation which one day we easily cast off, another day as easily overpowers us. It may be the same temptation, but we are not the same; we are changed in outward circumstances — changed, perhaps, in health; our whole atmosphere is changed. When physically and spiritually strong, temptation is weak: when physically and spiritually weak, temptation is strong and resistance to it is pain.

Sin does not lie in the passions and appetites, but in the *will*. It does not lie even in the strength of the passions, but in the absence of a stronger controlling will: and Christ's sinlessness lay not in the want of the feelings natural to man, but in the complete subordination of these feelings to the higher feelings of a will perfectly at one with God. He had a perfectly human *love of rest,* and in that there was no sin; He needed rest. But when tempted to give up His Father's work for the sake of rest His perfect will cried, " I must work the works My Father giveth Me to do." He had a perfectly human *indignation at injustice and wrong* — witness His words: " Are ye come out as against a thief, with swords and staves, to take Me? " — an indignation that in any of us would pass easily into revenge: and He overcame the temptation by saying, " but the Scriptures must be fulfilled." He had a perfectly *human shrinking from shame and dishonour* — a shrinking, therefore, from the disgrace attaching to a crucifixion -death. In that there was no sin. But when tempted on that account to refuse the Cross, He conquered by the faith that said, "Not My will but Thine be done."

In all this He "learned obedience by the things He suffered "; learned the pain that must often be involved in obedience where weak men are concerned; learned it as He could not otherwise have done, by actual participation in their weakness. When tempted to relieve His hunger by an act of disobedience and distrust, or when tempted to secure the homage of the crowd by proclaiming Himself an earthly king, there was really no risk of His yielding to the temptation, for His perfect will beat only in harmony with the will of God; but he learned, by enduring the temptation, how hard it must often be for weak men, whose wills are not perfectly attuned to God, to overcome: how hard the struggle must sometimes be for those who see that earthly gain will be the result of some specious sin, while righteousness brings no reward on earth at all, but only suffering and tears, and who, seeing this, are, in a moment of temptation, sorely perplexed, and scarce know how to escape defeat. The " suffering " under temptation thus gave Him a new power of *experimental* sympathy with suffering men. He gained the advantage of being able to sympathise with the painful struggles of His brethren, while He had not the disadvantage of being Himself overcome: for He was tempted, *"yet without sin."*

Does it seem strange to call His sinlessness an advantage to His sympathy? Do we think it would have been better for us if He had known something of

26

defeat? If even once He had been overcome, would not that have brought Him nearer to us, and made us more assured of His sympathy in *our* defeats?

But we are called to the Throne of Grace to obtain *mercy,* and not merely a sort of indulgent or easy-going indifference to our falls. What kind of sympathy is it that we need in Him to whom we lay bare the secrets of our hearts, and who is our Judge, as well as our Brother Man? Does the fact that a man has fallen before temptation make him better able to adjudicate faithfully between the claims of Righteousness on the one side and Mercy on the other? Not so. It makes him weakly indulgent rather than mercifully kind.

It has been well remarked that there are two classes of men quite unfitted for being judges of others: those who have never been tempted, and those who have fallen. Men who feel no temptation whatever to certain sins are often severest in condemning those in whom the tendency to these sins is strong. They are unmerciful because they have never been tempted. But men who have fallen before temptation are equally unfit to show mercy. They are lenient enough, but it is not a holy leniency, only a weak indulgence. Their maxim is, " Human nature is terribly weak and terribly corrupt; sin can hardly be helped; we must say little about sin, and take men as they are." There is only One who can hold the balance steady between unfair severity and unholy leniency; because, though He felt temptation's power, He came forth from it unsubdued: and hence it is that God has " committed all judgment " to Christ, "because He is the *Son of Man.*"

It is infinitely encouraging this thought of the tempted but victorious Christ. It makes the secret place of prayer a place of trustful rest to a weary sin-tempted heart. Going into it to speak to such a Lord, so infinitely holy and yet so infinitely tender; our Judge and yet our Saviour, our King and yet our Priest; Divine, and therefore able to read us thoroughly —human, and therefore able to sympathise with us all the time, we can go boldly to the Throne, and find it not merely a Throne of Justice, but a Throne of Compassion, a Throne of *Grace.*

> "Birds have on all green trees their nest,
> Foxes their holes, and man his bed:
> All creatures have their quiet rest, —
> Thou hadst not where to lay Thy head.
>
> And yet, Lord, Thou didst come to give
> Thy weary-hearted children rest,
> To bid the mourning sinner live,
> To soothe the aching, troubled breast.
>
> Oh! since on earth Thou lovest best
> To dwell in souls that mourn their sin,
> Come! take Thine everlasting rest
> This broken, contrite heart within!"

- Anon.

27

"The touch that heals the broken heart
  Is never felt above:
The angels know His blessedness.
  But way-worn hearts His love."

- P. B.

IX - The Blessedness of a Broken and Contrite Heart Realised When We Are Alone with God

IF it is when alone with God that we realise the whole extent of our sinfulness, till the heart is broken with the shame of it, it is there too that we can best hear the whisper of peace from a sin-forgiving God, by which the broken heart is healed. For we cannot parade a broken heart. It shuns the unsympathetic glare of day. If we carry it on the face, and ask every one to pity us because of it, that only proves that it is not really a broken heart at all. But we can tell the Divine listener about it in the secret place, and feel that such a heart "He will not despise." He will pity it, and heal it too. In the secret place we learn this wonderful fact, that a broken heart is what God delights to see!

There are not many things He delights to see in a broken condition; but this is one of them. He has no delight in seeing broken promises, or broken vows, or broken commandments, or broken restraints. These are the very things He charges against us, to prove how sinful we are. But there are some things that are best in their broken condition. It is from the broken earth that the harvest springs, from the broken cloud that the rain distils, from the broken alabaster-box that the sweet perfume flows. It is by broken grain that man is fed, and by the broken life of Christ that everlasting life is ours. We sing of Him, " Bread of the world in mercy broken." His own words are, " My body broken for you."

When the truth about everything now dark is at last revealed, it will be seen how precious in God's sight have been many broken things; how broken hopes for this world led to the better hope of heaven, broken earthly fortunes to the winning of eternal riches, broken health to the heahng of the soul. But chief among all these precious things is the broken heart, a heart that has lost all its hardness and pride, a heart that is humbled to the dust in penitence and prayer, a heart that no longer lifts itself up in self-sufficiency, but lies contrite at God's feet, a heart to which sin has become the most bitter of all bitter things, and deliverance from sin the highest blessing of which it can conceive.

What often goes by the name of heartbrokenness has little or nothing to do with the consciousness of personal sin. It might rather be called heartwretchedness. The spirit is broken by the troubles and disappointments of life; but that is all. There is nothing sanctifying in a misery such as that: often the very reverse. It produces a sullen discontent which sometimes rises to

28

wild complainings against the world and against God Himself. That is " the sorrow that worketh death." Real heartbrokenness for sin is a different thing altogether. *It* " worketh repentance unto salvation "; it is a " sickness that is not unto death, but for the glory of God, that the Son of God may be glorified thereby."

No wonder, therefore, that " a broken and contrite heart He will not despise." How can He despise what He has been at infinite pains to bring about? The whole purpose, both of His providential dealings outwardly and of the strivings of His Spirit within, is just to bring down the hard self-sufficiency of the heart that rebels against His law, and puts aside His grace; and to force from it the confession, " I am a sinner all over, a sinner all through ": and if He perseveres in this work till the result is reached in a completely *' broken and contrite heart," how can He but rejoice to hear its self-accusations and to see its tears?

It is a wonderful change that comes over any man when, instead of flattering himself and praising himself as he used to do, he can honestly speak of " abhorring himself." It is a radical change that. It is no mere surrender of the outposts. It is the fall of the citadel. It is not a reform merely; it is a revolution, and the very revolution God has been making and waiting for.

It is a striking proof of God's delight in a broken heart that whenever He means to bring His largest and most enduring blessings to any of us He begins by breaking us down. It often costs much to have this done. The process is pain, but the blessing is sure.

There is a legend somewhere which tells how a certain wilful Franciscan monk refused most stubbornly to obey his superior's commands, and how a severe but suggestive discipline was resorted to, to break down his will. His brethren dug a deep perpendicular grave, placed him standing in it, and began to fill in the earth. After a few shovelfuls were thrown in he was asked, " Is your will dead yet? " but there was no response from the iron heart. So the burying process went on, and the same question was repeated as the earth reached, successively, his loins, his breast, his neck: but the stubborn heart would give no reply. Remorselessly the earth was thrown in again. It reached his lips. In a few moments more they would have been stilled for ever. But then the iron will broke utterly. The submissive friar meekly answered, '* I am dead."

How hard the discipline is that is needed to break down the heart in penitence before its God, many a man from his own experience can tell. But it is worth the pain. A *breaking* heart is not a happy heart: but the reason of that is not that some of it is broken, but that so much of it is still unbroken and whole. When broken thoroughly, it becomes a happy heart at once: for — strange but true — it is only when completely broken that it is completely healed.

There was a remarkable law connected with the cleansing of the leper: " The priest shall consider, and behold, if the leprosy have *covered all the flesh,* he shall pronounce him clean that hath the plague." Has not that a spiritual meaning for ourselves? Our Divine Priest waits till our sense of our own corruption is so deep that we confess " from the sole of the foot even to the head there is no soundness in us," before He can say to us, " Go in peace and be whole of thy plague ": for —

> "Let our debts be what they may, however great or small,
> So soon as we have nought to pay, our Lord forgives us all;
> 'Tis perfect poverty alone that sets the soul at large,
> While we can call one mite our own, we have no full discharge."

But, just as the leper was " shut up alone " when this discovery of his condition was made, it is when alone with ourselves that we come to see our utter sin; when alone with God that we come to realise His utter grace, and through that grace to get our instant release. So long as we forgive ourselves, we are not forgiven by the Lord. When we utterly condemn ourselves. He says to us, " Be thou clean."

It is strange how men, with the Bible in their hands, persist in thinking that God will accept what, a thousand times over, He has declared, in the plainest terms. He cannot accept. There are multitudes of professedly religious men, who, if they gave an absolutely honest statement of their hopes for the hereafter, would point complacently to their general uprightness, tbeir freedom from gross sins, the kindly affections of their social and domestic life. They really go to God with a claim of right founded on virtues which half the tombstones of the world attribute to all that sleep beneath them! They never had any deep sense of personal sin, never uttered a really heartbroken cry for pardon, never were disturbed for an hour by any self-condemnation; and yet they have no doubt of a rightful place in God's heaven at last. What a terrible surprise to such men will be the first moment after death — when they find that that heaven is filled only with broken hearts, and a broken heart is a thing they never knew.

Why has God such delight in the broken heart? First, because He gets His right place within it, the only place He will ever consent to fill. Secondly, because Christ is adequately valued only by the broken heart. What a glory weeping eyes can see in Jesus of Nazareth and Calvary! The poor broken-hearted thief upon the Cross saw more in Him than all the self-satisfied scribes and Pharisees could do. "He came," says Pascal, "to heal the sick and let the healthy die." Thirdly, because the Word of Life is so precious to the broken heart. "I have learned more within these curtains than from all the books I ever read," said Richard Cecil on his bed of suffering: and why? just because he read the Bible there, not as a critic, nor as a controversialist, nor even as a minister for the sake of others, but simply as a sinner, a broken-hearted man. And fourthly, because as the Hearer of prayer " the Lord is nigh to them that are of a broken heart." There are no prayers like the prayers of the broken heart. No "princes" have such "power with God" as broken-hearted men. Jacob, in one night of broken-hearted wrestling with God, gained more than he had gained by the feebler prayers of half a century.

One great defect, surely, in the religion of the day is that there is not enough of the broken heart in it. Oh for more! and, in order to that a larger acquaintance with the secret place where God, in showing us ourselves, shows us *Himself* as well.

"Thy works, not mine, O Christ,
Speak gladness to this heart;
They tell me all is done,
They bid my fears depart.

Thy Cross, not mine, O Christ,
Has borne the awful load
Of sins, that none in earth
Or heaven could bear but God.

Thy death, not mine, Christ,
Has paid the ransom due;
Ten thousand deaths like mine
Would have been all too few.
        To whom save Thee,
            Who can alone
            For sins atone.
    Lord, shall I flee?"

- H. Bonar

"O my Redeemer, who for me wast slain,
Thou bringest me forgiveness and release;
Thy death has ransomed me to God again,
And now my heart can rest in perfect peace."

- Spitta.

X - A Burdened Conscience Soonest Gets Relief When Alone with God

IF it delights God to see a thoroughly broken heart bending low before Him, to heal that broken heart delights Him yet more: and so, into the secret place where we wait to hear His voice, He comes and says, " When men are cast down, thou shalt say, there is lifting up," and He shows us what the up-lifting is.

It was when the troubled company of conscience-stricken disciples were within the shut doors of the upper room that the Risen Lord came in and said, " Peace be unto you." That was a wonderful greeting, for they were not merely in terror of their lives; they were in remorse of conscience for their cowardly forsaking of Him; and He meant it not merely to calm their human fears, but to bring them such joyful news as had never gladdened them before. He was speaking to them from the other side of the Cross than the one they were thinking of, from the heavenly side both of the Cross and of the grave: speaking not merely as the absent Friend who had come again to them, and come without any upbraiding of them for their sin, but as the Great Conqueror who had overcome, and whose triumphant "It is finished " had laid the foundation for a peace between them and God which nothing evermore could shake. His message, " Peace be unto you," was far more than just a kindly greeting. It meant, "I have made full atonement for you on the Cross, and the atonement has been ratified in heaven, for I am risen from the dead; I bring you peace with God, and assure you of it."

In the quiet of the shut doors of our homes and hearts He brings the same message to those who long to hear it. It is often the very message we most need to hear. For we so often and so easily lose the sense of peace with God. We fall under the power of temptation, and darkness comes between ns and Him. We feel our sins to be great barriers between Him and us that we cannot overleap. It will not do to silence our consciences. They only speak the louder for the attempt to smother them: and there is an infinite difference between a conscience *pacified* and a conscience merely *benumbed*. The deep cry of the broken heart is not for cosmetics to give the appearance of health, but for a cure that will reach the very seat of the evil, and purge it thoroughly. And God meets the cry, just by bringing us back to the *simplicities* of the Gospel of His grace. There is no other way.

Any peace that does not honestly face our personal guilt, that either ignores it, or denies it, or excuses it, is not worth seeking for. It cannot last. For the very first condition of peace between us and God is a settlement of His controversy with us about our personal sin: and till we get that sin forgiven, cancelled, put out of the way, His controversy with us must go on. But sin can be forgiven only at the Cross of Christ. The only answer to a guilty conscience is, " Christ has died ": and the simplicity of the Gospel message is its pointing to that one glorious fact, and telling us that if we want peace with God we must think not of some righteousness of our own to be made by constant effort as perfect as we can make it to be, but of the already perfect Righteousness of God's Christ which may be ours for the taking, if only we stretch out for it an absolutely empty hand.

John Bunyan tells how, walking alone in the fields, crushed by the misery of an accusing conscience, he seemed to hear a voice above him that said, " The Lord our Righteousness " — and how, immediately, the thought flashed into his troubled soul, "It is righteousness God wants in me to take me into heaven; well, if Christ is my righteousness, then my righteousness has been in heaven, and God has been looking at it, for sixteen hundred years "; and so he came out of the darkness into the light of a perfect peace. It is only so that peace can come to any man: for what God gives us through His Son is not *salvability* merely, but *actual salvation;* not just the hope of acquittal hereafter, but full acquittal here and now, *immediate* peace through "the one sacrifice for sins for ever" offered on the Cross.

We need to be continually going back to that Cross to read the *fourth* inscription written on it. For there were four, though Pilate intended there should be only three. He wrote, in contempt for the Crucified, a threefold inscription which was visible to every passer by: but all the time God's unseen hand was writing a fourth inscription there in eternal praise of the Crucified, but which only the eyes of faith can see. Millions have gazed upon the Cross as it blazed on splendid altars, or glittered on priestly robes, or shone on cathedral spires, and yet have not seen this Divine inscription on it. Millions have marched to battle under the standard of the Cross, and yet have not seen it. Millions wear the Cross as an ornament upon their dress, and yet do not see it. But to the eye of faith it stands out as clear as the rainbow did against the cloud of judgment: and that Divine inscription is the one foundation of all our peace. It is this, "God, in Christ, reconciling the world to Himself, not imputing their trespasses unto them," "making Him to be sin for them who knew no sin, that they might be made the righteousness of God in Him."

There is certainly more in the Gospel than just the doctrine of the Cross: but that lies at the foundation of all else. And though there is a sense in which we ought to get beyond the Cross, even as Christ did, and rise like Him into new and free and glorious life, there is also a sense in which we can never get beyond the Cross, but must come back to it, and linger at it, again, yet again, if our peace is to be full. It is a simple truth this, too simple for many, but in its very simplicity lies its power.

It is good for us to look much at the living Christ. We do not look at Him nearly enough as an Example and a Friend. But our soul's rest must still be the sacrifice of Calvary. A stimulus to holiness we can find in His life: the cleansing of our conscience we can find only in His "Blood." The Crucified Christ must be the Alpha and the Omega of all our peace with God. To live in settled peace with Him we have to do with the " atoning blood of Christ " what Rahab did with the scarlet cord that was to her the pledge of safety — so place it that wherever we may look it may meet the eye. She fastened the scarlet cord in the window of her house, and could not look out in any direction without looking across it. Let us place the atoning blood in the window of the soul, so that, whether we look earthwards or heavenwards, it may every day remind us wherein our peace with God must lie; the great atonement made on Calvary, once for all.

There are few professed Christians to whom Christ's atonement is not *something,* but fewer still to whom, as the basis of hope, it is *all.* Some make Gods of their own. Some make Christs of their own. And some *make half-*

Christs. They make Saviours, or half -Saviours, of their repentances, their good resolves, their benevolences, their integrity, their prayers. As they lie on dying beds they look over their past lives, not completely satisfied, but half satisfied: and, scraping together all the good they can find in themselves, they bring in Christ to eke out their deficiencies and make up the rest.

How many have yet to learn that a half-Christ will not do — have yet to learn to spell "works" and "grace" without mingling the letters — have yet to learn that the " robe of righteousness" is not patchwork, partly theirs and partly His, but must be His alone! The message of the Gospel is not that Christ came to help the weak or subsidise the imperfect, but *"to save the lost."* And if it is one glory of the Gospel that it tells of *salvation "without money"* it is an equal glory of the Gospel that it tells of *salvation without delay.* "Being justified by faith we *have* peace with God through our Lord Jesus Christ."

The same Cross that shows the exceeding awfulness of sin, since no blood could expiate it, and no death pardon it, but the blood and death of God's own Sinless and Beloved Son, shows also the exceeding riches of His grace that asks no penance from us ere forgiveness comes, but pardons freely and pardons at once. And thus the Cross makes us at once the lowliest and the joyfullest of men — lowly, because our sin we never can forget, joyful because God has forgotten it for ever.

"Now when Christian came up to the Cross, his burden loosed from off his shoulders, and fell from off his back, and tumbled into the sepulchre, and he saw it no more. Then he gave three leaps of joy, and went on, singing —

"'Blest Cross I Blest sepulchre! blest rather be
The Man that there was put to shame for me.'"

"Lord, gather from the regions dim and far,
   Desires and thoughts that wander far from Thee;
To home and rest lead on, guiding star, —
   No other home or rest but God for me!

To Thee my heart as incense shall arise,
   Consumed upon Thine altar all my will;
Love, praise, and peace, an evening sacrifice,
   In Thee, my Lord, I rest, and I am still."

- **Tersteegen.**

"O'er the waves that cannot rest,
   O'er the drifting foam.
Wandering dove without a nest,
   Weary-winged I come.

Still and sweet the silence deep
   Where no foot hath trod;

Softer than an infant's sleep
Is my rest in God."

- Tersteegen.

XI - The Troubled Heart Comes Quickly to Quiet Rest When Alone with God

A VERY beautiful name is given to Christ when He is called "The Lord of Peace." He is the Great Peacemaker, for He has "made peace by the blood of His Cross"; and He is also the Great Peacegiver, for He says, "My peace I give unto you." Bringing to us, first of all, peace of conscience, and teaching us how to look up to *God* without fear. He brings us, next, peace of heart, and teaches us how to look out upon *the world* without fear. By His Cross He makes us satisfied with God's way of saving us; by His life He teaches us to be equally satisfied with God's way of REST training us. He brings us into His own perfect calm by showing us how to live, as He Himself always did, with an absolutely unquestioning trust in a Heavenly Father's love.

Those hours and even days of restless worry and anxiety about earthly things that so often come to us — how utterly unlike they are to the habitual feelings of Jesus Christ! Not one single instance can we find in which He sought to have His earthly lot changed from what His Father had appointed it to be, or complained because He could not change it, or made Himself miserable by anticipating the sorrows that were lying in front and ready to fall.

We are constantly criticising God. Christ never did. Even though not actually criticising Him, we are yet constantly imagining that things might, somehow, have been better arranged for us than they are. When any crushing sorrow falls upon us, the rebellious heart, if not the lips, will say, "I could have borne this if it had only come to me at some other time — if it had come alone, instead of being accompanied by so many other depressing circumstances — if it had been of a different kind, failure in my business instead of failure in my health, a stroke upon myself instead of upon my child, the loss of some other friend than just that one that was the best-beloved of all," and so on through a hundred suppositions of what might have been better arranged. How seldom do we realise the faithlessness that is in such a mood of soul as this!

But we may come to realise it, and escape from it too, if, in the secret of His presence, alone with Him, we lay our burdens at His feet and listen for His words of peace. For, as we listen, He will tell us much.

He will tell us that the whole explanation of the severity of the trial (in our view of it) is that our desires and His purposes are not moving in the same line, that we have not the same idea of life that He has, otherwise there would be no *disappointment* in us with the pain that life may bring; that if we are making it our chief aim in life just to have a prosperous time of self-indulgence, while His aim is to train us, all along life's way, to holiness of character and heavenliness of spirit, there is sure to be collision everywhere between our wills and His, and that not till this collision ceases can we get the peace we long to know.

He will tell us, therefore, that what we need is not that the world should be changed to us, but that we should be changed to it; that, in all our plans and ambitions, we should no longer put first what He puts only second, and no longer put second what He puts first and wants us to put first as well: that it is a complete change of *centre* that is needed, and that where that change is made there will be an instant change all round the circumference too.

In the secret of His presence He will tell us more. He will tell us that if we rebel against our trials it is only because we do not see His planned issue of them in our greater good: that they are only a Great Refiner's fire for the purifying of His gold, a Great Vine-dresser's knife for increasing the fruitfulness of His vines. He will whisper to our crushed hearts in the secret place, "What I do thou knowest not now, but thou shalt know hereafter."

It is only the eye of the sculptor that can see beforehand the finished statue in the rough marble-block; but he does see it, and all the strokes of his tools are meant to bring out to the eyes of others what is already clear to his own. And the strokes of God's hand are only to produce the perfect beauty of the soul, and make that as visible to others as it now is to Himself. Nothing is more certain than that we will be perfectly satisfied with His work when we see it finished. Why should we not be satisfied now when He tells us what a glorious finish He will make, and leave to Him the choosing of the tools?

Very beautifully was this thought once pressed home on one who was in acute distress because of a long succession of calamities, when, happening to visit a ribbon-weaving factory, he was shown a new machine for producing fabrics finer than any seen before. He examined it carefully; but, skilled mechanician though he was, he could not understand how the work was done. Finding that all the movements of wheels and levers and threads were controlled by some arrangement in a central box kept closely shut, he asked to be allowed to look inside, but was told, " The master keeps the key." These simple words were like a flash of heavenly light into his darkened soul. " Here is my life," he thought, " full of what seems to me inextricable confusion; what the meaning of its cross-purposes may be I cannot tell: but if in me the Divinely perfect pattern is at last wrought out, I need not ask on what principle my God is fashioning me for His glory, "My Master keeps the key."

Perhaps, if all were known, it would be found that the majority of trustful disciples in every age were made so by means of the heavy afflictions and sadnesses of life; God darkening the glory of this world to force them gently to look to a glory that is not of this world at all. "Tears are our telescopes to let us see farther into heaven." God washes the eyes with tears till they can look undazzled on the land where tears are known no more.

36

Then, once again, the Lord will remind us in the secret place that exemption from suffering is not what He ever promised us, but only victory over it, and sanctification by it, and peace along with it: and therefore exemption from it would be a loss and not a gain; for as it is the water that dashes against the mill-wheel that keeps the mill in motion, the incessantly beating trials of life keep grace in the soul alive. It is said that migrating birds, preparing to wing their flight to summer climes, wait for a wind that blows against them, for that assists them to rise to the needed elevation; and the things of which we often say, "All these things are against me," are the things of which God says, "They are meant to help you to soar."

The one universal heart's ease, therefore, is to let a loving God take His own wise way with us. Doing this willingly, we will no longer torment ourselves with speculations as to how our sorrows have come, or why they been permitted to take the special form that makes them so hard to bear. Our only feeling will be the feeling of Christ Himself, whose peace we have come to share, " The cup which My Father hath given Me, shall I not drink it?"

Our gracious God promises us more than sympathy alone when we lay our sorrows at His feet: He promises us help as well. But we must leave to Him the way of helping us. Many a time we distress ourselves needlessly by refusing to rise above our fears till we see *how* the help is to come, and in what precise way we may look for an answer to our prayers. We want God to explain to us the secrets of His working before we feel certain that He will make things go right. But there is something better than *understanding* God, and that is, *trusting* Him. He does not promise to *explain* Himself. He does promise to *reveal* Himself: but He never reveals Himself except to an absolute trust.

When a little child awakes at midnight, startled and crying because of sounds it knows not the meaning of, how is it comforted and pacified? Is it by a scientific explanation of the sounds? by a lesson in meteorology or natural history? Is it not rather by the mother taking her trembling little one into her arms, and soothing it there to sleep, till it thinks no more of the sounds that troubled it, or of any explanation of the sounds, but only of the mother in whose sheltering embrace it lies?

So God takes up each trembling child of His, and makes it feel safe simply because He is holding it: and what comforts it is not what it knows about its troubles, or about the way in which the trouble will be kept at bay, but what it knows about Him in whose strong and loving arms it lies enwrapped. In this there is infinite peace. It is just by drawing us to Himself in absolute trust that He changes our restlessness into rest: and the calming whispers of His love can be heard nowhere so distinctly as in the secret place of quiet fellowship, where we are alone with Him. The oftener we are there, the more of His peace we shall know.

"Hath not each heart a passion and a dream,
Each, some companionship for ever sweet,

And each, in saddest skies some silver gleam,
And each, some passing joy too faint and fleet,
And each, a staff and stay, though frail it prove,
And each, a face he fain would ever see?
    And what have I? — a glory and a calm,
    A life that is an everlasting psalm,
    A heaven of endless oy in Thee."

- Tersteegen.

XII - We Rise into Fellowship with Things Unseen When Alone with God

IT is good to do this, even for a single hour. It gives us a loftier view of the great purpose of life, and a calmer view of the discipline of life. It shows us the infinite compensations that take the sting out of the sorrows of life; and it is the only thing that can do it. Sequestered thus from the "pride of man," and from "the strife of tongues," we learn to feel about everything as Christ felt, who lived habitually above all the ordinary ambitions of men, and accepted the deepest humiliations of life as willingly as a worldly heart would accept a throne.

It is one of the choicest blessings of the secret place where we are alone with God, that there we can so fully enter into fellowship with the Unseen; a fellowship that enshrines the very root-idea of the Christian life. What is a Christian? Can a better answer to that question be found than this: " He is one who is living by faith on an unseen Saviour, who surrenders himself absolutely to the dominion of an unseen Lord, who acknowledges the mastery of an unseen hope, who yields himself to the attraction of an unseen power"?

And yet how difficult it is to live in the realm of unseen things! The remoter attraction of the unseen is neutralised by the nearer attraction of the seen. The needle of a ship's compass is so adjusted that it may swing free of the attraction of its immediate surroundings, and, by being unaffected by the motion of the vessel, may respond to the control of an unseen power, the great magnetic current that runs from pole to pole. It is meant to yield itself to this unseen power alone; but it can respond to the unseen only when loose to the seen. And what our souls need is such an adjustment of their relations to the world on the one hand, and to heaven upon the other, that, be the fluctuations of their immediate environment what these may, they will respond easily to the great attraction of the skies.

But this is not habitually the case, even with good men. They are like a compass so rigidly bolted to the timbers of the ship that every movement of the vessel seriously affects it. When the sea of life is calm — in the hush of Sabbath rest, in the sanctuary of worship, in the chamber of prayer, in times of good health and outward prosperity — the needle points right enough to

God and heaven. But sorrows come, disappointments come, reverses of fortune come, sickness comes, temptation comes, and immediately all is wrong; the needle points neither to faith, nor patience, nor peace. Their Christian graces come out only "weather permitting." Their souls have indeed been touched by the Divine magnetism, but that influence does not get free play. What they need is that their too firm attachment to things seen should remorselessly be broken, so that the power of the unseen may be free to act; and where can this connection with earth be more effectively cut than in the stillness of the soul when alone with God, and the world is for the time shut entirely out?

The value of this absolute surrender to the unseen is found most emphatically when trouble of any kind has to be met and overcome. Surely the great Apostle was sitting quietly alone with God when he looked out upon the seething tribulations of his life, and said, "None of these things move me." Surely he was very near to God when he wrote down his triumphant verdict upon the sufferings of his lot, " Our light affliction which is but for a moment worketh for us a far more exceeding and eternal weight of glory, while we look not to the things that are seen, but to the things that are not seen; for the things that are seen are temporal, but the things that are not seen are eternal."

Christian men of an earnestly spiritual type are sometimes accused of too much " otherworldliness "; of living too much among unseen and eternal things, despising things seen and temporal. The truer charge against most Christians would be that they have too much of "present worldliness," that they do not think half enough of the eternal that so far transcends the temporal. One of the ancient philosophers divided men into "earthly" and "winged" souls. Alas! the "earthly" souls are many, and the "winged" souls few. Accused of soaring! God pity us that we so seldom soar at all, and never high enough. Even Paul could not *always* soar. Even he could not always feel his sufferings to be " light, and only for a moment." He could do that only " while he looked to the things unseen and eternal." God's all-sufficing peace can come into us in no other way. If this steady look to things above is wanting, our looking at things below will be either terribly dispiriting or terribly ensnaring.

But the clear upward look enabled him to reverse entirely the judgments he would naturally have passed on things below. What he would naturally have called heavy, he calls " light "; what he would otherwise have fainted under because seeming never to end, he calls " but for a moment "; what might have been thought only a visionary hope, a phantasm of the imagination, a dream, he calls a " weight of glory." And he can scarce find words to express his full sense of its greatness; it is for him not only " glory," but "a weight of glory," "an exceeding weight of glory," "a more exceeding weight of glory," "a far more exceeding weight of glory," "a far more exceeding and eternal weight of glory." The scales of the balance in which he weighs his troubles and his compensations are not in equipoise. One of them is immeasurably heavier than the other; and so he feels that "the sufferings of the present time are *not worthy to be compared* with the glory that shall be revealed in us."

Could we but let into our souls the grandeur of this thought, our conclusion would be just what Paul's conclusion was — that all passionately absorbing pursuit of earthly honours, distinctions, gains, is not, as it is commonly held to be, a wise thing, but supremely foolish, for "the things which are seen are only temporal"; and that the intensest pursuit of spiritual riches is not, as the world reckons it to be, a foolish thing, but supremely wise, for " the things that are unseen are eternal."

If at any time we are planning great things for ourselves, laying out our future, so as to secure for ourselves something like a paradise below, we have but to remember that *' the things that are seen are temporal," and that will sober our poor ambitions at once. If we are mourning too dejectedly over losses in the past, casting regretful looks upon vanished joys till a spirit of bitterness almost crushes faith, we have only to remember again that "the things seen are temporal," and that will reconcile us to their loss. We have but to write under our longest list of earthly treasures, either lost in the past, or possessed in the present, or expected in the future, the one word " temporal," and the almost magical effect of realising that fact will be a quick killing both of our foolish ambitions and of our sinful regrets. And if, going on to write out another and a brighter catalogue of the things that God has prepared for us, and is keeping for us, to be given us in due time, we put under it or over it the one word " eternal," the magical effect of realising that fact will be the perfect peace that keeps both heart and mind, enabling us to say, "Well, if God is going to give us so much that is glorious ere long, we may willingly let Him send us a little that is grievous now."

We need often to do in secret fellowship with God what every prudent man of business does frequently when alone with his books — make out a spiritual balance-sheet, a careful profit-and-loss account. Vague impressions of our spiritual solvency should never content us. We ought, for our heart's peace, to have the matter made absolutely clear. This was what Paul evidently did, for we hear him say, "I *reckon* that the sufferings of this present time are not worthy to be compared with the glory that is to be revealed." "I have made the calculation," he says, "I have patiently worked it out." He does not say, "I believe that that is so"; or, "I take for granted that it may be so "; or, " I am trying hard to feel that it is so." But he says, "I have accurately estimated all the elements of the case, I have set the eternal over against the temporal in every possible light, and by rigid reckoning I find this to be the result. I have brought Divine arithmetic to bear upon the case, and I am as completely sure of the accuracy of my conclusion as I am that two and two make four." If this were to us also, not a conjecture merely, or a hope, but a conviction founded upon a calm and deliberate calculation, the conviction would be a triumph, and the triumph would be a song.

And there is really no place where the great calculation can be so easily and so unerringly made, as the secret place of fellowship with unseen things, where we are alone with God.

"Come to our poor nature's night
With Thy blessed inward light,
Holy Ghost the Infinite,
        Comforter Divine!

Like the dew Thy peace distil,
Guide, subdue our wayward will,
Things of Christ unfolding still,
        Comforter Divine!

In us 'Abba, Father!' cry,
Earnest of our bliss on high,
Seal of immortality.
        Comforter Divine!"

- Rev. G. Rawson.

"Why should the children of a king
    Go mourning all their days?
Great Comforter I descend, and bring
    Some tokens of Thy grace.

Assure my conscience of her part
    In the Redeemer's blood;
And bear Thy witness with my heart
    That I am born of God."

- Isaac Watts.

XIII - We Can Hear Most Distinctly the Witness of The Spirit When Alone with God

THE voice of the Holy Spirit is low, and can be heard distinctly only in the silence of the soul. It is always a "still small voice," easily lost amid the clamour of the noisy world. But we need to hear it. However varied and even unwelcome sometimes its messages may be, we need to hear them all: but He will speak to us words of comfort only if we do not turn away when He speaks words of warning and reproof.

Sometimes He speaks to us in our indifference as a "Spirit of judgment," convincing us of our sins. Sometimes He is a rebuking Spirit, making us ashamed of our deficiencies, and humbling us to the dust. At other times He comes into our darkness as the "Spirit of Light "; into our perplexities as the "Spirit of Wisdom "; into our ignorance as the "Spirit of Truth "; into our fears as the "Spirit of Peace"; into our weakness as the "Spirit of Might "; into our deadness as the "Spirit of Life." As the " Spirit of Grace and Supplication" He helps us to pray; as the "Anointing Spirit " He consecrates and empowers us for service; and as the "Spirit of Adoption" He enables us to realise our sonship to the Father, for the "Spirit Himself beareth witness with our spirit that we are the children of God."

This is one of the most comforting and gladdening services the Holy Spirit renders us. But what is this " witnessing with our spirit "? And how is the witness borne? In connection with this subject there has always been a large amount of mystical and even fanatical talk; men who were consciously living in gross sin, boasting that they had an inward witness telling them that they were true children of God. But even without going so perilously far as that, many devout and humble Christians greatly distress themselves by concluding that since they never heard any such voice proclaiming their sonship, they must be unworthy to hear it, and cannot be the children of God at all.

It must be noted, therefore, that Paul speaks not of one single witness testifying to us a truth which is to be credited on that testimony alone, but of two independent witnesses, whose united witness-bearing can alone prove it to be a truth. He speaks of the Holy Spirit bearing witness, not *to* our spirit, but *with* our spirit: and these two really bear witness to different things. Our own spirit bears witness to *facts* which we know, and the Holy Spirit bears witness to the *meaning* of these facts.

As thus: I sit down with the open Word of God, which shows me the characteristic marks of a soul that has been renewed. My own spirit tells me that these characteristic marks can be found in me. I am conscious of a transforming change in feeling and in life. Though I am not all that I ought to be, nor all that I might be, nor all that I hope to be, still I am very different from what I once was. My affections Godward are changed for the better, ray ambitions are changed, my life, too, is greatly changed. Sin does not gratify me as once it did. The world does not satisfy me as once it did. New emotions are now stirring within me, new longings take possession of me. The Bible is a delight. Prayer is a joy. I long for holiness as I never used to do. I surrender myself to Christ as once I never did. He is really all to me. I can conceive no higher blessedness than to be with Him and like Him for ever. These are simple *facts* of my own experience and consciousness. I know them to be so. And the Holy Spirit interprets to me the *meaning* of these facts. It is that I have been "born again," for "all things are new." And thus He "bears witness *with* my spirit" that I am a child of God.

This is really the whole secret of "assurance of salvation." There is nothing mystical in it. By the new Godward feelings that stir within ourselves we come to realise our true relationship to Him who has been the sole Author of them all. We know the fact of our sonship because the feelings of sonship are within us, even though we have sorrowfully to confess that our filial love and filial trust and filial obedience fall lamentably short of what they ought to be.

The case is this: if I want to know whether God is calling me one of His sons, I ask myself, " Can I look up confidingly and call Him my Father, feeling Him to be so indeed?" If I want to know what His feelings towards me are, I ask myself, " What are my feelings towards Him? Can I look up into His face with the joy of a trustful child and say, 'Abba, Father'? " That was how Jesus felt. But if " Abba, Father " was the cry of the Son, it is also the cry within me of the Spirit of the Son, for He puts it into my heart to say the same. I can never say that, in all the fulness and intensity of its blessed meaning, unless He teaches me to do it: and so I am assured of my sonship, not because it is a conclusion of my own mind, but because all the time that I am saying, almost tremblingly, "I think I am a child of God," He whispers in my heart, "You are so in very deed."

This explains how assurance may ebb and flow; may be weaker at one time and stronger at another. If we sink back or down into any kind of sin, either of the flesh or of the spirit, there can no longer be an honest witness within ourselves to our possession of the characteristics of a child of God; and the Spirit being " grieved " by our declension refuses to bear witness to our sonship. His witness to the *meaning* of the characteristics is still the same as ever; but now that witness stands alone; the witness of our own hearts to the possession of them is silenced; " our hearts condemn us, and we have no confidence before God ": there is no bearing witness *with* our spirit that we are sons.

The peace of God within us is a delicate plant, and is easily killed by the frost of sin. It is a precious treasure, but is easily stolen by the secret hand of some thievish iniquity. God will indeed " speak peace to His people," but "let them not return to folly," otherwise His voice will be dumb.

An old writer says: "If any one living an unholy life were to tell me that he has an inward Divine assurance of everlasting life, I would not believe him though he brought an angel from heaven to corroborate his assertion; for the peace of God is holy peace, and in an unholy heart it cannot dwell." If God's commanding voice is not obeyed. His comforting voice will not be heard. "Grow in holiness, if you want peace to grow in you."

We thus see the one cause of all our disheartening variations of hope. The holier we are, the stronger our assurance is: the more careless we are, the weaker it is. Only we must remember that it is not the mere presence of sin in the heart that proves us to be not children of God. It is the persistent love of sin, and its dominion over us, that proves that. Sin lives in every Christian, but no Christian willingly and habitually lives in sin. It may be his tormentor and enslaver, but it is not his chosen Lord. It is not really a part of himself, but only a hateful parasite from whose gnawing and enfeebling presence he would fain be free.

To say that an imperfect or faulty Christian cannot be a son, even though his imperfection is a sore affliction to himself, is only like saying of a cripple, "This cannot be the heir, because he is so deformed," although the deformity is to him a daily pain. But, on the other hand, if he were not deformed as he is, but full of strength and grace, the doubt founded upon his deformity would never arise. If we were only more holy, if our likeness to the perfect Christ were only more clear to ourselves as well as to others, it would be more evident to ourselves and to others also that we really belong to Him: and the voice of His Spirit witnessing with our own would be more distinctly heard.

For the hearing of that voice there is no time like the still hour when we are alone with God. If we are often there, the secret place where we lay open all the heart to Him will be a place where deepest joy will mingle with deepest penitence — "the voice of rejoicing and salvation" with "the voice of our weeping." We shall assuredly see our sins there. Even our "secret sins" will be "set in the light of His countenance" there: but He will tell us, as we confess them at His feet, that they are sins *atoned for,* and sins *forgiven;* and so "a peace that passeth understanding will keep our heart and mind by Christ Jesus."

"Lord, what a change within us one short hour
Spent in Thy presence will prevail to make!
What heavy burdens from our bosoms take,
What parched grounds refresh, as with a shower!
We kneel, and all around us seems to lower;
We rise, and all, the distant and the near.
Stands forth in sunny outline, brave and clear;
We kneel, how weak! — we rise, how full of power!
Why, therefore, should we do ourselves this wrong
Or others, that we are not strong,
That we are ever overborne with care,
That we should ever weak or heartless be,
Anxious or troubled, when with us is prayer.
And joy, and strength, and courage are with Thee?"

- **Archbishop Trench.**

XIV - We Can Best Renew Our Strength by Being Much Alone with God

EVERY disciple of Jesus Christ is called by His own commissioning and consecrating words, to be in the world what He Himself was from first to last, a true witness for God. "I have ordained you to go and bring forth fruit;" "As My Father sent Me, so send I you." We are to bless the world by our very presence in it, as well as by our labours for it. But this we cannot do unless our strength for service is perpetually renewed; and it is only from much secret fellowship with Christ that the renewing of our strength can come.

For He tells us unmistakably that for any union with Him in *service* there must first be union of *life*. He speaks of Himself as the Vine, and of His disciples as its branches: but the whole fruitfulness of the branches depends upon the closeness of their vital connection with the Vine. It is the life that is in the Vine flowing freely and continuously into them that alone keeps them in a fruit-bearing condition. If our power as witnesses for God in the world is small, the reason of that is given by the Lord Himself, " Cut off from Me, ye can do nothing." We *give out* so little, only because we *take* so little in.

The interdependence of the Vine and the branches is very wonderful. *Without the branches the Vine can do nothing.* If His disciples do not bear fruit, then, so far as the blessing of the world is concerned, He lives in vain. But *without the Vine the branches can do nothing.* If they cease to bear any fruit, or if their fruit is poor, it is because the flow of His Divine life into them has been checked, or has altogether ceased. All that the Vine possesses is for the use of the branches. The Divine riches of grace are not stored up in Him for Himself, but for them; to be communicated every day and every hour to each separate branch, that it may use them for His praise, and so prove the truth of the words, " From ME is thy fruit found." For larger fruit-bearing, therefore, we must live in far closer and more intimate connection with Christ than we usually seek.

There is an expression used by Paul which contains an idea somewhat unfamiliar but very suggestive. He speaks of "growing *into* Christ." That is more than growing into the likeness of Christ. It is growing into increasing closeness of personal union to Christ. The whole Christian life is a growing *out of* Christ, as the branch grows out of the stem: but that outward growth is conditioned by, and proportioned to, an inward growth, a growth farther into Christ, as the branch, the farther out it grows, grows also farther in, its fibres taking ever a firmer hold of the stem. There is a *deepening of their insertion,* as well as an extension of their spread. But this constant deepening of connection with Christ, who is our life, is a secret thing, a process unseen by any eye except God's. Our outward growth and fruit bearing are the only things that can be seen of men: but whereever this outward growth is, it is the result of an inner process that cannot be seen, the soul taking, in secret, an ever firmer hold of Christ, becoming more and more closely bound to Him by faith and love, and so receiving more uninterruptedly the power for serving Him. That process is one that always goes on best in our secret hours of heart-fellowship with the Lord: indeed, it can hardly well go on anywhere else. Were it continuously going on, what mighty Christians we might become!

It may be taken as an axiom in the Christian life that all our best and most strengthening experiences come to us when alone with God. *Jacob* was thus alone when, at Peniel, he wrestled with the angel, and got his new name, Israel, and could then go out to meet his angry brother Esau without any fear.

Moses was alone with God in the Midian desert, when the voice of the Great I AM commissioned him and fitted him to be the leader of his whole nation out of bondage into rest. It was also from lonely fellowship with God in " the secret place of thundering " on Sinai's top, that he brought away the wondrous glory on his shining face that awed the people into obedience to Him from whose radiant Presence he so unmistakably had come.

Elijah was alone with God at Horeb when, after being humbled to the dust, he was girt with a strength for his great work such as he never had before.

It was when alone with God in the silent spaces of the Syrian deserts that *John the Baptist* was endowed with the wondrous power that made his preaching of repentance bend the multitudes as trees are bent by a winter's gale.

It was in the still deeper solitudes of Arabia that *Paul,* alone with God, away from all disturbing old associations, away from all human teaching, listening only to the voice of God, was trained to become the noblest Apostle of the Cross.

It was in the solitude of intercourse with Christ on the Isle of Patnios, that the beloved disciple *John* got his wondrous visions of things to come. Shut out from the noisy world by the dividing sea, shut in with Christ, he saw what no other eye had ever seen, and heard what no other ear could hear.

And was not the *Lord Jesus* Himself prepared for His great redeeming work, not only by those forty days in the wilderness where He was "alone with the wild beasts," but also by His continuously-sought fellowship with the Father on lonely mountain-tops in the silence of the night, " the morning star finding Him where the evening star had left Him — on bended knees"?

To us also all our best experiences come when we are alone with God. There are sorrows which we can surmount in no other place. Grief is of many kinds, but all grief that is really terrible and heart-crushing sends us into speechless solitude to weep it out upon the heart of God. There are temptations which can be overcome only when alone with Him. The fight with the great adversary is a single combat after all. And there are deep joys that can come into us only when alone with God, the joy of feeling Christ's personal love, the joy of finding His strength made perfect in our weakness, the joy of bringing our empty vessels to the Divine fulness of His grace, waiting till he fills them, and seeing them overflow. For quickening faith, intensifying love, and renewing strength, there is no place like "the secret of His Presence." Strange and sad that we do not seek it more!

For the strength will not come to us without our going deep to find it. A few hasty and lazy prayers will never bring it into us. We need *deep* communion with Christ if we are to get it at all. There is no part of a tree so *invisible* as its roots: but none more essential to its growth and fruitfulness: and just as the visible condition of the tree is an unfailing index of what the unseen roots are doing, our visible lives will soon tell whether or not our invisible roots are going deep: for dryness below ground soon means deadness above ground.

Jeremiah explains the vigour and fruitfulness of God's trees by a most suggestive metaphor, "They *send forth* their roots to the river." God provides the water: and there is more than enough of it for our need: it is a "river" — but we have to "send forth our roots" in search of it. Large trees can survive a drought that withers smaller ones, because their roots go deep, and find sources of moisture that are never dry: and a strong, well-nourished Christian is proof against temptations and trials that wither feebler souls, just because his roots go deep into the water of life. He draws strength out of deep heart-intercourse with God, out of the secret study of the Word, out of private prayer; but these things he has to seek: he must go in search of the water, for the water will not come to him.

There is a celebrated vine at Hampton Court that for many years disappointed the gardener's hopes. It was quite healthy, but there were few grapes. One year, however, it was unexpectedly laden with clusters of the finest fruit. Seeking to discover the cause of this, the gardener laid bare its roots, and traced their ramifications, and found that they had suddenly gone through the banks into the river Thames. It had "sent forth its roots to the river," and thenceforth "ceased not from yielding fruit." That is a parable for all of us. If we are to bear fruit in large abundance we must get access to the hidden resources of God's grace that are waiting for us to tap — and that is a secret process, a secret between us and God alone. Without this deep fellowship, this secret communion with the Unseen, there will be no growth for any of us: but with this, and because of this, there will be abundant fruit — fruit even to old age. And He who is the Unseen Giver of what we unseen receive will be glorified in us who are thus "enriched by Him unto all bountifulness, causing through us thanksgiving unto Him."

"How good It is when, weaned from all beside,
With God alone the heart is satisfied!
How good the heart's still chamber thus to close
        On all but God alone,
There, in the sweetness of His love repose,
        His love unknown!
To hear His voice amid the stillness blest,
And lay me down upon His arm to rest!"

- **Tersteegen.**

XV - We Are Lifted Easily Above Life's Discouragements When Alone with God

To be always hopeful and courageous in depressing circumstances is not an easy thing. The discipline of life seems often very hard; and we rebel against it, not because of its hardness alone, but because much of it seems so unnecessary. Sometimes it is the pettiness of our ordinary life that weighs us down: and sometimes it is the disappointing ineffectiveness of our efforts to serve God worthily. Our ordinary concerns look so poor and mean that we long to be free from them, so as to spend life in a nobler way; but we cannot get free: we are chained to the drudgery; we cannot rise. "This endless struggle just to live," we say, "this weary round of uncongenial work day after day, this endless buying and selling, this ceaseless toil of mere housekeeping, this narrowing down of my thoughts to the petty details of food and clothing; this irksome monotony of life, where I have the same small things to attend to day after day, all the year through, unable to get above them or devote my energies to loftier things — why does God tie me down to a life like this? Why does He not give me work to do in which I could better serve Him, and at the same time better satisfy my own idea of what a noble life ought to be?"

If we take such questionings to God in the still hour of meditation and prayer, however, we shall get His answer to them clear enough, just as He gave it to Israel by Moses long ago. He will tell us that what we call the drudgery of our common days is meant to do two great things that are absolutely indispensable, first "to humble us," and next "to prove us, and to see whether we will keep His commandments or no."

It needs not only Divine *teaching,* but Divine *discipline* in addition to the teaching, to make us content with faithfulness in very lowly things, instead of complaining that we have not greater things to do. We are eager to do great things. Our pride and self-complacency are flattered by our having large services demanded of us. And God understands us well, and therefore seeks to purge us of this pride by giving us only common and humble things to do, that ostentation may not tempt the heart.

But the discipline is also meant "to prove us" whether we will keep His commandments or no"; to see whether we are seeking simply to do *His* will, and are not pursuing our own. There is hardly one man in a thousand who sets himself steadily and humbly just to do the will of God with no ulterior aims whatsoever. If we all did that, there would not be a single unhappy heart in the world! In our impassioned longings for some other kinds of life than what is God's present will concerning us we are living in the region of dreams; and men are not sanctified by dreams, but by battles. When that old people of Israel listening to God at the fiery mount had a bright vision of the great and noble life they would enter on ere long, they thrilled with devotion to Him, and vowed perfect obedience to His will in everything. But how long was it till they were bitterly complaining of the tiresome and poor monotony of those wanderings in the desert by which the vision was to be realised? And where are our vows of obedience too? Where are our professions of living only according to His will? To have bright visions of what a noble thing life might be made to be is not to make it so. But all the time we are looking at our dream-pictures, God is taking a better way with us, though we see not what His meaning is — training us to humble faithfulness by the seeming drudgery of commonplace duties in an uncongenial sphere: and He shows us this as soon as we get alone with Him.

There is another and a keener discouragement, too, over which nothing can lift us so easily and so completely as a quiet talk with God — the discouragement arising not from the pettiness of our lives, but from our disappointing ineffectiveness and want of success in working for God's righteousness in the world. The discouragement grows often into despair, and we cry, "Oh that I had wings like a dove, then would I fly away and be at rest!" That was the cry of a thoroughly dispirited man, yet not a worldly man, nor a man simply saddened by accumulating sorrows; rather, a man weary with the vain struggle against the opposing forces of evil, a man striving to fight against the sin around him, and to put down iniquity, yet finding his efforts thwarted on every hand, and almost giving up the battle in despair, saying bitterly, "I have spent my strength for nought and in vain. Can God mean that His work shall be only pain to me and defeat? Has He nothing better to give me than this?"

There are many such hearts in the world to-day; earnest Christian hearts, zealous for God, yet saddened by the feeling that all their efforts are in vain; not world-weary, nor sin-weary, nor sorrow-weary, but battle-weary; looking at the difficulties on every side, thinking of their own weakness to stem the rushing tide of evil, and looking forward to the long-drawn fight that is before them still, till their courage fails, and they shrink from the depressing prospect of useless battle to the very last. For it is not the sharpness of the conflict, but the weary length of it, that often makes the heart give way. It is the never-endingness of the fight, the hopelessness of anticipating any triumphant close, that makes so many who are really soldiers of the King cry, " Oh that I had wings like a dove, to fly away and be at rest!" and who that feels any true sympathy with Christ in His mission to the world can help being sometimes depressed by the seeming futility of all the means used by faith and love to gain the world for Him?

But now let this depression be not nursed in the brooding mind, but taken into the secret place of communion with God, and how soon a different complexion is put upon the circumstances that cause it! What has *He* to say about it? What is *His* answer to the weary sigh? It is just *to think of Christ*. Who had ever so sore a fight as He, or more discouragements than He? Who ever kept up the fight to the very last as He? It was said of Him before He came, " He shall not fail *nor he discouraged* till He have set judgment in the earth," and

He has fulfilled the prophecy. He has been waiting for His victory for nineteen hundred years, and is waiting for it yet, but waiting undiscouraged as well as undismayed, " expecting till His enemies be made His footstool." The unfailing and unfainting hopefulness of Jesus Christ may shame us out of our discouragement while following Him as " fellow-workers with Him unto the Kingdom of God." The one answer to all our despondency is — Christ. If *He* had spoken as we so often speak, and felt as we so often feel; if He, seeing how small His success was, had folded His weary hands and given up the conflict, *what then?* And what was *His* review of His life when almost done? "I have glorified Thee upon the earth, I have finished the work Thou gavest me to do." That was all, but that was enough. Can any of us wish to be able to say more? "Oh for wings," we cry, "to fly away and be at rest!" But if Christ had said that, where would our redemption have been? Wings await us only as they awaited Him — only when, like Him, we have finished the work given us to do, and have fought out the battle to the end. *Armour* now; *wings,* if we are patient, we shall find in due time.

Yet, even meanwhile, the blessings of "wings" is not always denied; not wings with which to escape all troubles, but wings with which to rise above them. "They that wait upon the Lord shall mount up on wings as eagles; they shall run and not be weary, they shall walk and not faint." That is not a promise for the far-distant future. It is a promise for the present; and each part of it will be at one time or another, fulfilled to the "waiting" heart. There will be soaring days, when we get so high above the world that we can feel as if we had parted company for ever with its sorrows and its temptations, when we can not only *outrun* the vexations of life, but *outfly* them, and feel as if they did not exist. God means us sometimes to have hours like these; but they are not the *ordinary* experience even of the best of men. The ordinary experience is a lower, and yet equally comforting one — the fulfilment of the other part of the promise, "They shall run and not be weary; they shall walk and not faint." Not so ecstatic an experience as the soaring, but quite as useful and possibly more safe, is this humbler experience given to those who know that they have no might in themselves, and wait for God's might to strengthen them.

And the order of these three promises is to be noted well, for they are often fulfilled to us just in that order and no other. It may seem strange that the loftiest attainment should be put first and the lower last; but this order is the true one for all that. The soaring days of every Christian generally come at an early stage. At the wonderful time of his "first love," his first experience of the riches of Divine grace, his conversion days, he often rises wonderfully high above the world. Never, indeed, does he feel so completely loosed from its thrall, never does he rise to such a height both of joy and of surrender; his glowing feelings seem then to carry him up to the very gates of heaven.

But soon he has to come down from his ecstasies because God calls him to battle and service below, and then he learns to be thankful if only he can " run with patience the race set before him."

And later still he is humbler still. A larger experience of the world and of himself shows him that constant "running" even is a thing he cannot keep up. He is thankful then if he can but "walk" with God, leaning upon His everlasting arm, till he comes to the dark valley at the end of the pilgrim way, and finds that there is no soaring over it, nor running through it. He is glad of the Lord's staff to keep him from falling, and will only say, " Yea, though I *walk* through the valley of the shadow of death I will fear no evil." But as he goes leaning on God he finds that God's strength gives him the victory as completely as when he was able to soar.

Now, the manifold discouragements of life are sure to oppress us terribly so long as we are merely *alone with ourselves,* and brooding over them; but they will quickly disappear when we are *alone with God;* for then we look upon them with *His* eyes, weigh them in His balances, measure them by *His* tests; and as we review them in *His* light there comes into us a great hope, a great courage, and a great peace.

"A moment from this outward life,
Its service, self-denial, strife,
    I joyfully retreat:
My soul, through intercourse with Thee,
Strengthened, refreshed, and calm shall be,
    The world again to meet."

                                                                    - "The Changed Cross."

"Oh! to be but emptier, lowlier.
    All unnoticed and unknown;
But to God a vessel holier.
    Filled with Christ, and Christ alone."

                                                                    - P. Gerhardt.

XVI - We Discover the Source of All Power for Service When We Are Alone with God

IF we are discouraged by our conscious inefficiency as witnesses to God and workers for God in the world, we must, before all else, discover the cause of our inefficiency: yet this is what we find it often difficult to know. Our weakness we painfully feel. Others see it as well as ourselves; but what the cause of it may be, or how to get it removed, we cannot tell.

There is only one place where these questions will be solved — the secret place where we lay ourselves freely open to God's searching eye, and where we wait longingly and humbly to hear what He has to say: and the solution gained there will probably be this, that, while we are complaining that we are too weak to do much for God, He shows us that, in reality, we are *too strong* for Him to use; we do not feel weak enough, or so conscious of our own weakness, as to cast away every rag of our own self-sufficiency, and wait for the power of God Himself to come upon us, and qualify us for serving Him. We need to have Divine power, and not our own human power, behind all the actings of the life, and all the words of the lip. We need to have this Divine power pouring into us if it is to pour forth from us again: and this inpouring of Divine power is given only when we are in stillness waiting for it, and pleading for it, and claiming it from the Lord according to His promise.

Let our natural powers of mind or tongue be what they may, we are quite unfit for serving God till the power of His Spirit comes upon us to consecrate the power that belongs to ourselves. Indeed, till this Divine power comes, we have really no power of our own for any spiritual work, even the smallest and humblest of all. But we almost never realise this thoroughly; and consequently, it is not our weakness but our fancied strength that is the great hindrance to our being used by God. All dependence upon our own wisdom, our own talents, our own intellectual grasp, our own powers of argument or persuasion or appeal, ignores the fundamental truth that " our sufficiency is from Him."

When a steamship has grounded on the sand bar at a river's mouth, its own power is valueless for moving it. So far from helping it, the energy of its own machinery will only strain and injure it. What then? It must *wait for God's power,* the power of the rising tide. That great uplifting force will do easily and quickly what its own internal power cannot do; and this is but a parable of human helplessness waiting for the power that is Divine.

How many a preacher knows that this is his only resource! How often, when he thought his prepared message as powerful as reasoning and oratory could make it to be, it was utterly useless, and had no real spiritual effect on a single hearer's soul! but when he painfully felt his own utter weakness, and was willing to be only the channel along which a Divine power should flow, even though his message seemed to himself so poor that he was half ashamed to speak it, God did use him as he had never been used before! All our natural powers can be used mightily by God; but only when we think nothing of *them,* and surrender ourselves to be simply the vehicles of Divine power, letting God use us as He wills, content to be even despised by men if He be glorified.

It may be said, therefore, with confidence, that the cause of our inefficiency in God's service is threefold. First, *we are not still enough* for God to come to us. Secondly, *we are not empty enough* for God to fill us. Thirdly, *we are not sanctified enough* for God to use and honour us.

There are two suggestive Scripture metaphors, among many others, that show this very clearly. One of these is that which likens the coining down of the Holy Spirit upon us to the falling of the dew. Another is that which likens the Christian to a vessel fashioned by the Lord Himself, to be filled by Himself, and used in whatsoever way He Himself may choose.

1. We need to be still enough for God to come to us. The gracious influence of the Holy Spirit falls upon the soul just as the dew falls in the stillness of the night upon the drooping plant. The plant cannot make the dew: it can only wait for it, and attract it. The dew is always close beside it, suspended in the atmosphere; but it does not fall unless two conditions are fulfilled — *the air must he still, and the plant must he cool.* We need much quiet stillness of soul if the grace of the Spirit is to come down out of heaven and revive us; and the fever-heat of life, too, must be suffered to abate, for the blessed baptism, giving power from on high, can descend only when the heart is cooled as well as still.

2. Then, again, we need to be empty enough for God to fill us. Paul, writing to Timothy, gives in a beautiful way God's idea of what every true and faithful Christian ought to be, "a vessel unto honour, sanctified and meet for the Master's use, and prepared to every good work." The metaphor is a very exalting one, but a very humbling one as well. It tells us the high dignity to which we are called — to be "vessels to honour" in the Lord's "great house." It tells us what our high service in the great house is to be — "prepared unto every good work." But it tells us also what in a moment takes down any pride of self-sufficiency — that we are only "vessels," that God fashions us as it pleases Him, and uses us as it pleases Him, that we have nothing of our own, but are merely His vehicles for receiving and carrying and distributing what He fills us with.

But the difficulty and the hindrance on our side often is that we are not willing to be this and nothing more. We are not always self-emptied enough to let the "Master" of the "great house" put into us what He wills, and use us as He wills. It is a wonderful honour to be vessels in His hand. It is altogether marvellous grace that can take what were once only "vessels of wrath," transform them into " vessels of mercy," and then make of these vessels of mercy "vessels to honour," vessels fit for the noblest use, vessels filled with the grace which they may carry to other souls. But do we realise that, after all, we are only vessels — vessels of various sizes, some of them "vessels of cups," and others "vessels of flagons" — vessels of different make, some of them plain and unadorned, others enriched with carving and colouring of the finest kind — vessels of different materials, some of " gold and silver," others of "wood and earth" — vessels to be employed in different ways, some of larger usefulness than others, some constantly in use, others in use only at occasional times — but all of them only vessels, empty vessels till He fills them, vessels to be used by Him in any way He thinks best, or to be laid aside upon the shelf if He has no present use to put them to? Do we always realise and consent to this? Do we not sometimes feel perfectly willing to be His vessels, if only He will make us great enough and ornamental enough to satisfy ourselves; if only He will fill us with all aromatic spices instead of common water; but not willing to be of meaner make, or to be used in a less self-glorifying way?

3. We need to be holy enough for God to honour us. " Vessels unto honour " are " sanctified " vessels, vessels " purged " of evil within, vessels hallowed and consecrated for His service alone. This is the most essential characteristic of all. How can the Lord of purity use uncleansed vessels when He wants to carry in them the "pure water of life" to some thirsty lip, or the wine of the kingdom to some fainting heart?

The measure of our Christian power is just the measure of our Christian consecration. A single unmortified lust, whether of the flesh or of the spirit, a single besetting sin tolerated in heart or life, will hinder all our usefulness to God, even though we be vessels of the most beautiful ornamentation and of the finest make.

"Take away the dross from the silver, and there shall come forth a vessel for the refiner," is one of Solomon's pithy sayings; and in its spiritual application it goes very deep. Does it not mean, "Take away all conscious defilement from soul and life, and then, as hallowed vessels, God will be able to use you for His praise "? It was a law for ancient Israel that they should "bring an offering *in a clean vessel* into the house of the Lord." If unclean, it would be only " a vessel in which is no pleasure," and the offering within it would not be accepted at His hands. That law is one that still stands unrepealed in the statute-book of Christ.

These are some of God's answers to our questionings about inefficiency in service, and they are sufficient to be both a rebuke and a stimulus when we listen to them in the secret place where alone they can be heard. It was just at the very time when Saul of Tarsus was in the depths of self-condemnation and self-despair, utterly emptied of all his former self-sufficiency, that the Lord Jesus said of him to Ananias, "He is a chosen vessel unto Me, to bear My name before the Gentiles and kings, and the people of Israel." If we could only begin with a self-emptying as he did, might we not end where he did too, "filled with the Holy Ghost"?

> "Nearer yet, O Christ, still nearer
> To Thy heart of Love!
> Lift me higher, knit me closer
> To the things above!
>
> Fuller still, Christ, still fuller
> Be my joy in Thee!
> Stronger every day, still stronger
> Thy rich grace in me!
>
> Clearer yet, Christ, still clearer
> Be the vision fair
> Of the holy unsoiled garments
> Saints in glory wear!

Holier still, Christ, still holier
   Be my walk below!
Help me onward, raise me upward,
   Liker them to grow.

Brighter yet, O Christ, still brighter
   I for Thee would shine.
Make me now, and make me ever,
   Altogether Thine."

- Anon.

XVII - Our Holiest Aspirations Are Intensified When We Are Alone with God

ONE of the great discoveries we make when we rise for a little while above the blinding and depressing mists of life's anxieties and cares to the serene pure air of the mountain-top in the secret place, is that ordinarily we are living much lower down than we might live and ought to live; that we do not appropriate the fulness of God's grace as we might do; that we might be far happier and far holier than we generally are. It is in the quiet of the still hour that we hear most distinctly the call to seek a higher life, a life of higher experience, of higher aims, and therefore of higher joys.

We ought to rise higher *in experience.* How much of the *fulness* of Divine grace we know almost nothing of! How much belongs to us in Christ that we have never claimed as personally our own! To say that it is the privilege of every Christian to enjoy to the utmost the blessings that flow to him from his union to Christ is not to say enough. It is more than his privilege. It is his duty as well. We not only may be, but ought to be, " strengthened with all might by His Spirit in the inner man," "abounding in hope," "kept in perfect peace." But do we really seek this? Do we actually attain it? Is it uncharitable to say that most Christians are only barely alive? Their spiritual pulse is feeble; their spiritual progress is slow; their spiritual victories are few; their spiritual joys are poor. There is no vigour in their faith. If they see at all it is only dimly. The full sunshine they never know. The clouds hang always low and trail heavily across their sky.

This poor and meagre experience is certainly better than no experience of grace at all; just as a sick man is better than a dead man. But when Christ comes to do His saving work upon us, He does not restore us from death to sickliness; He restores from death to the fulness of happy life. Why do we not enjoy the assured position He gives us? Why do we walk so often with drooping face and downcast eye when Christ has risen a Conqueror, to make us sharers in His triumph over sin and death and hell? Looking upon our gloom covered faces, listening to our cheerless, half faithless tones, who would ever dream that we were the heirs of a glorious liberty obtained for us by the

Christ who died, and rose again, and lives for evermore?

When Jesus came out of the grave He did not bring the grave-clothes with Him. Lazarus did, and many Christians do. They walk about really "risen," but with the smell of the sepulchre clinging to their garments. They have "life," but they have not "liberty." The reality of life they have, but the joyousness of the new life they do not show. Why should it be so? The full peace He gives we need for our own soul's sake; and we need it for the sake of our power to win the world. We cannot by our life tell powerfully upon others if we are only gasping for life ourselves. The well of peace within ourselves must be full to the brim before it can overflow in blessing all around. We cannot draw others out of the pit of gloom if we ourselves, though a little higher up than they, are still trembling in precarious safety as we cling to the slippery stones.

It is good to be penitents at God's feet, but it is better to be consciously restored penitents lying in the Father's arms. Tears for sin are good, but praise for the Hand that wipes the tears away is better. The cry of the publican, " God be merciful to me a sinner," was good, but the song in his heart as he " went down to his house justified " was better still. It is good to " sit down in the lowest room," as though unworthy of a higher place, but better far to hear the Master say, " Friend, go up higher," and then " to sit with Him in heavenly places " without any misgiving as to our right to be there.

A large number of earnest -minded Christians do long to be able to rise to this, but their deeply-felt unworthiness of it is a difficulty they cannot surmount. That is just because they are living too far from the Christ in whom they faintly trust. If we understood more fully the reason of His love, we would see that it is quite independent of our worthiness to receive it. Discoveries of our sinfulness may take *us* by surprise, but our sinfulness is no surprise to *Him.* He knew from the very first what our unworthiness, in all its length and breadth, would be, and yet He loved us — loved us for reasons in Himself alone. So, then, if He began to love us for His own sake, not for ours, He can go on loving us for His own sake still. If He had loved us at our best, and came to be disappointed in us, His love might grow cold and even cease altogether. But He loved us *at our very worst*, loved us when "dead in sin," loved us knowing all we would turn out to be; and the one word "grace" explains the wonderful fact. Our hope rests not upon our own steadfastness in faith and perseverance in holy living, but on unchanging everlasting grace; the same grace that began in love ending in love as well.

We ought to rise higher *in expectancy* too. "Grace after grace" is what He promises, but only "according to our faith" will the grace be given; and they who bring the largest pitchers to the fountain take the largest blessing away. The less we expect from the world the better; the less we expect from ourselves the better; but the more we expect from God, the richer, the holier, the happier we are sure to be. Surely He must take it ill that we expect so little when He says, "Open thy mouth wide and I will fill it." We ought to expect to have every one of His promises fulfilled to us, however great it be; and what we need for that is not a stronger faith so much as a faith that is simpler and more childlike.

Above all, we need to rise higher *in fellowship with God*. This is "a high hill as the hill of Bashan," but none can climb too high upon it. What a wonderful elasticity of spirits is felt by one who has got to the crown of some grey peak! what a feeling of utter calm and of superiority to things below! We pity those who have never felt the exhilaration of the mountain air. Any one who gets high up upon the holy hill of fellowship with God is sure to feel the same. If the cares of the lower world disturb us, we have but to climb this hill and we are at once in the serene calm of heaven — a calm that neither care nor sorrow can invade. If the temptations of the world overpower us, it is because we are living too far down. If higher up we would be beyond the tempter's voice.

High fellowship with God will make us radiant too as well as calm and safe. The light of heaven will linger longer on our souls. In the Alps, when darkness has crept down into all the valleys, bright light can be seen bathing the giant peaks that catch the glory of the descending sun, and retain, when lower ones have lost it, the glow of its expiring flame. Then, when the glow has fled from even the loftiest pinnacles of ice, it can be seen reddening the clouds that are higher yet, till they look like the garments of angels flung off upon the golden sky. These also lose their light ere long; but if we could ascend beyond every cloud, and beyond the shadow of the earth itself, we should have the full sunshine always without a break.

So if we want our souls to be transfigured, and our lives ennobled by the perpetual sunshine of God's presence, where no sorrow can enshroud us and no sin can live, we have but to seek higher fellowship with Him in His secret place, and live more delightedly among "the things that are above."

"Welcome, dear Book! souls' joy and food,
In thee the hidden stone, the manna lies;
The key that opens to all mysteries
The Word in characters, God in the Voice."

- H. Vaughan.

"Tree of life, thy golden-fruited
  Branches shade as well as feed,
  By the stilly waters rooted;
  And thy very leaves drop healing
  Medicine in my hours of need.

  When my soul is vexed with sorrow
  Like a sea, it groweth calm
  When thou speakest; Hope's to-morrow
  Cheers to-day, and to my trouble
  Thou art soothing balm.

Paradise of fadeless pleasure,
Stored with mines of wealth untold,
Ind is not so full of treasure,
Ophir is not richer: thou art
More to me than gold."

- Rev. Richard Glover.

XVIII - The Bread of Life Is Sweetest When We Are Alone with God

IN the secret place we need to do far more than speak to God. We need to listen as He speaks to us: and we hear His voice in the Sacred Word which conveys a message from Him to every one who "has ears to hear." Do we really prize this book of God as we ought? Do we really know it? Do we treat it as He means it to be treated? Do we make it our souls' daily food?

Few things are more amazing than the ignorance of this blessed Book that is discoverable in thousands who call themselves by the Christian name. It is no breach of charity to say that there are multitudes in all the Churches who never open their Bibles except once a week in the house of worship, and even there betray by unmistakable signs how ignorant of its contents they are. They would be ashamed to be as ignorant of the newspaper or of the last novel as they are of the Word of God. An allusion to Bible-story has more than once set half of the House of Commons wondering where it came from. We can easily tell, when talking with any one about Divine things, whether he has much converse with the Divine Book or not. Men of the world, keen, well-educated, well-read in current and ancient literature, skilled in many abstruse departments of human research, often make fools of themselves when they talk about spiritual realities; and that simply because they never read the only book that speaks authoritatively about these realities. The Bible is not only a sealed book to them, it is like a dead book altogether.

These days of ours are far less Bible-searching days than former ones, even within our recollection, were. Religious literature, not to speak of secular, has come almost to displace the Bible, even in Christian homes. Family reading of the Bible, and instruction in it, is getting to be a thing of the past; and from this, more than anything else, comes the current laxity of belief and of practice too.

We are sometimes told that we make too much of the Bible: that we worship it too much: and that idolatry of the Bible is as pernicious as idolatry of anything else: and in saying this, it is implied that this is a too common state of things. But where are they, these idolaters? One would like to discover them, that he might go and live amongst them! For most men seem to make far too little of the Bible instead of too much. They read it too little; they study it too little; they believe it too little; they practise it too little. One would travel a long way to see a real idolater of the Bible; for there are not many of them near at hand!

To many the Bible is merely an antiquarian museum of curiosities; to others merely a storehouse of weapons for controversy. Some read it critically; some read it sceptically; some read it mechanically as if performing a task. How few read it as children in a far country listening to a letter from home! If it is to be of any real use to us, we must take it as God meant it to be taken, as bread for our hunger and water for our thirst, as medicine for our sicknesses and balm for our bruises, as a staff for our weariness, a spur for our indolence, a light for our darkness, a comforter in our sadness, a polestar for our wanderings, a lamp for our feet.

Of all these uses the most *essential* is the first. We need this Divine Word as the food by which alone our spiritual life can be sustained and grow. Many an enfeebled and diseased condition of body is accounted for simply by "insufficient nourishment"; and all spiritual energy and even vitality depends upon spiritual nutrition. Wherever we see a feeble Christian, we may be sure he is suffering from "lack of bread": and the two things needed for bodily nutrition are needed also for the nutrition of the soul.

One of these is a personal *appropriation* of the food. So long as the food remains outside of us — a thing to be looked at and admired, but not tasted — it does us no good. It must be taken m. "Thy words were found," says Jeremiah, "and I did eat them, and they were to me the rejoicing of my heart." We cannot eat by proxy. Eating must be our own personal food-appropriating act.

Then follows a further process — the *incorporation* of the food with the substance of the bodily frame. The food converted into flesh and blood reappears in the bright eye, the healthy complexion, the flexible muscle, the firm bone, the well-strung nerves, the active brain: and if the Word of God is really appropriated, it becomes incorporated too, and reappears in "love, joy, peace, longsuffering, gentleness, goodness, faith, meekness, temperance," and all the other characteristics of a strong and healthy soul.

All of us, without exception, need daily food: the old as well as the young, the strong as well as the weak, the king as well as the beggar (for " the king himself is served by the field "), the philosopher as well as the child. And the act by which life is nourished is as simple in the case of the philosopher as in the case of the child. If the wise man will not stoop to that simple act, he will die as surely as the child will who refuses food. And there is no man, however learned or however great, that can keep in spiritual health for a day if he will not nourish himself by the bread that endureth to everlasting life.

But no hasty, indifferent, surface-reading of the Divine Book will give any nourishment to the soul. An ancient Bible-lover said, "I will meditate upon Thy statutes." That is something deeper than merely listening to them. We need to ponder them till they are felt to be distinct personal messages from

God: and as Augustine said, comparing the Bible to the water of life, " there are first draughts, and second draughts, and third draughts of this water to be enjoyed." It is often only the third, and even the fourth, draught that proves how sweet and how refreshing it is. But this "meditation" needs silence. "Only in the sacredness of silence does the soul truly meet with the secret, hiding God," the God who reveals Himself in the Word, but also veils Himself under it, and can be seen only when the veil is thinned to transparency by that heavenly light that, like the mystic light of the Holy of Holies, shines only in "the secret place of the Most High."

What "meditation" does can be seen in such glad utterances as these: "Oh! how I love Thy law!" "It makes me wiser than all my teachers." "It is sweeter to my taste than the honeycomb." "It is better to me than thousands of gold and silver." And every humble, spirit-taught lover of Scripture still will heartily echo these words. But love for the Word will grow as our experience grows. There is much in it we never see till our own experience of life makes it a living book to us: and just as a letter written in " sympathetic " ink is illegible till exposed to the heat of the fire, many of God's wonderful messages are never understood till the fire of suffering brings out the message clearly to the eye of faith. Many a man has never known what the Bible can do for him till he has taken it down and read it tearfully on some dark day when the light of his home was gone, and by the fireside there was only an empty chair.

This is our own human experience; but was there ever one who knew the Scriptures better, and more delighted in them than Christ Jesus did? They were more deeply in His heart and oftener on His lips than any other had them before or since. And yet He never possessed a copy of His own! Scarce any child in a Christian home but has a Bible of his own. We have all our favourite copies, and delight to mark them with our private marks, and carry them about with us for constant reference. Christ had no such pocket Bible to carry about with Him, and yet no one knew it as He did. He had spent many an hour in the synagogues reading the copies that were there, and His holy memory did the rest, till He knew it so well that He never hesitated for a moment in using it either to defeat His foes, or to enlighten His disciples, or to comfort Himself: and it has been well said that " it is peculiarly enjoyable, in reading the Bible, to halt at some text, and know for certain by His quoting it, that out of the very vessel we are raising to our lips He Himself once drank the living water."

If any one could have dispensed with the Scriptures, He could, but none ever lived upon them more. He found everywhere in them His own portrait drawn — the Holy One, the humbled One, the rejected One, the crucified yet rising One, the suffering and thereafter glorified One; and He gave Himself to fulfil all that was written of Him there. We too must find our portrait in the Scriptures, the picture of what we are in our deformity and sin, the picture also of what God means us, through His transforming grace, to become: and we have to set ourselves to fulfil the high ideal of a sanctified life that is presented there. When we use the Scriptures as Christ did, they will do for us what they did for Him.

But for this sanctifying look into the Divine Word we do need the quiet of a silent hour. The full sweetness of the hidden manna can be tasted only when we are alone with God. Reading and pondering it there, we will find that, whether as an instructor in righteousness or as a comforter in sorrow, it has no rival anywhere. All other books at last grow insipid except this. It is the one book we carry into the chamber of the dying and into the home of the bereaved. If it were suddenly taken out of the world altogether, what a dismal void would be left in myriads of broken hearts! What millions of feet would wander into paths of deeper sin than have yet been trod! Knowing that nothing can take its place, our hands may well grasp it tighter every day, and our souls ponder it with fresh delight, till, in the light of God's secret heaven, we see and understand it all.

"I come to Thee to-night,
In my lone closet where no eye can see,
And dare to seek communion high with Thee,
        Father of love and light!

If I this day have striven,
With Thy blest Spirit, or have bowed the knee
To aught of earth in weak idolatry,
        I pray to be forgiven.

If I have turned away
From grief or suffering which I might relieve
Careless the cup of water ev'n to give,
        Forgive me, Lord, I pray!

Not for myself alone
Would I the blessings of Thy love implore;
But for each penitent the wide world o'er,
        Whom Thou hast called Thine own.

And for my heart's best friends,
Whose stedfast kindness o'er my painful years,
Has watched, to soothe affliction's grief and tears,
        My warmest prayer ascends.

Should o'er their path decline
The light of gladness, or of hope, or health,
Be Thou their solace, and their joy, and wealth,
        As they have long been mine."

- **Lyra Anglicana.**

XIX - All Selfish Feelings Are Expelled When We Are Alone with God

THERE is another privilege connected with the secret place of intercourse with God which must not be overlooked, the privilege of prayer for others as well as for ourselves. The prayer-chamber is to be a place of large intercession; and only if it be so is the full blessedness of it reached. Paradoxical seemingly, it is yet true, that when most alone with God, we must have many others beside us there. We must take our friends and brethren there; we must take all the sinful and sorrowful there; we must take the whole Church there; we must take the whole world there, and speak to God in behalf of all of these. This is a much-forgotten *duty,* but it is a greatly undervalued *privilege* as well.

God might certainly have limited our prayers to ourselves, just as we have to repent for ourselves, and believe for ourselves. That He allows intercessory prayer in addition to personal prayer is, therefore, a proof of the exceeding largeness of His loving heart, and of His desire to enlist all our natural feelings of sympathy on the side of His gracious purpose to bless as widely as blessing can go. For these intercessory prayers are a distinct means of drawing down blessing where, without them, it would not fall, or at least would be long delayed; and in this way we can reach many who are beyond reach of our words, or who would resent the words if uttered. The shortest way to many a heart in whose spiritual well-being we are deeply interested, but which constantly eludes our efforts to reach it by even the tenderest appeals, is round by the Throne of Grace, where we ask God to do for it what we cannot do. Hundreds of conversions and restorations have resulted from such secret prayers, prayers that those prayed for knew nothing of.

And it is not only for such great spiritual blessings to come to them that we ought to intercede. In tender human sympathy we ought to speak to God about their every-day life, their cares and dangers, their sorrows and their joys, and ask that His hand may guide them, His grace sustain them, His love cheer them, His Spirit sanctify them, and His power guard them from dangers we see close beside them but they do not. Few things are more delightful to a prayer-lover than thus to carry with himself into the Father's presence every friend he knows, to talk of every one by name, to lay out before God their special needs; and so to link them closer to himself as well as to his Lord by the sweet bond of prayer.

Such prayer for others will always have a salutary reflex influence upon ourselves. It will lead to a deepening of our interest in those for whom we pray, to wiser efforts for them, and to a greater watchfulness over ourselves, lest anything in ourselves should hinder the success of the prayer. And prayer for ourselves may sometimes remain unanswered, because it is selfish prayer. What Joseph said to Jacob's other sons in Egypt, God may sometimes say to us, "Ye shall not see My face except your brother be with you." It is significantly said at the end of the history of Job, "The Lord turned the captivity of Job when he prayed for his friends," the very friends who had cruelly misjudged him, and been bitter against him.

Then our secret prayer must take a wider sweep and embrace all the earth. We are to be God's "remembrancers," who "give Him no rest" till He has made His kingdom worldwide. It is for this that Christ is praying in the secret heaven; and we are to be "fellow workers with Him" in this as in so many other ways. An ever-interceding Christ above, and an ever-interceding discipleship below, are to be joined together in unfainting prayer till "His name is hallowed on earth as it is hallowed in heaven, His kingdom is come on earth as it is come in heaven, His will is done on earth as it is done in heaven."

But all this is easy work for the prayer chamber compared with another that lies equally upon us. To pray for personal relatives and friends, for fellow-Christians, for the whole Church, for the millions sunk in darkness and ignorance and sadness, and superstition and vice, is not so difficult as to pray lovingly for some living close beside us who treat us with contempt or with malevolence, and daily do us wrong.

It might be thought the very extravagance of charity to ask us to pray for our enemies, our rivals, our detractors, our persecutors, those whose evil tongues spread slanderous reports concerning us, whose bitter feelings towards us are never disguised, whose cold hatred meets us at every turn. But to pray for these is one of the most distinct commands of Christ, "Pray for those that despitefully use you and persecute you." He knew well what He was saying when He gave that command. He knew that it will be impossible for us to reciprocate their hatred and malevolence and contempt if we pray lovingly for them. He knew that the quickest way of overcoming their evil, and of preventing feelings of anger against them from overcoming us, is to pray for them in the spirit of Him who prayed for His very murderers upon the Cross. A good man once wrote in his journal these words: "Many a one would never have had a special place in my prayers but for the injuries he had done to me." That was the very spirit of his Lord. Wrathful feelings against those who treat us ill will often prevent prayer for ourselves being granted. "First be reconciled to thy brother, then come and offer thy gift," is a rule that may apply even to the presenting of prayers at the mercy-seat. If, therefore, at any time there seems to be a hiding of God's face, and the door of access to Him seems shut when we would enter in, let us try if the key of intercession *for others* will not turn the lock.

Then, too, the quiet of the secret place will help us to examine ourselves, to see if there may not be reasons on our own side for the ill-will in others of which we complain. If we are able, in this secrecy with God, to correct our too flattering judgments of ourselves, we are also able there to correct our too harsh, unsympathetic, and uncharitable judgments of others. We may carry our feelings of irritation against an offending brother to the door of the secret place, but it will be difficult to give them house-room within it. It has a wonderfully clarifying effect to look at what offends us in the treatment meted out to us by others, or in the feelings we suspect them to be cherishing towards us — to look at these quietly and seriously " in the cool of the day," and at the very time we are confessing our need of pardon for sins of our own.

Forgiveness of sin is the first blessing we receive when we come home to God. Renewed assurance of this forgiveness is what we seek as often as we bend in secret before our forgiving Lord. But we cannot have that assurance unless we are really forgiving our brethren as God forgives us — in the same generous forgetting way, and to the same extent — "not unto seven times, but unto seventy times seven." "If ye forgive not men their trespasses, neither will your Father who is in heaven forgive you"; and we can best learn this forgiving spirit in secret with the Lord, where, taking a calm review of the day, we look with uninflamed hearts at what, when the blood was hot, we construed as meaning studied slights, or insults, or wrongs.

For this correction of our own temper and dispositions towards offending brethren there is nothing like an hour of calm with God. The duty of cultivating a right temper we do not consider so much as we ought. Defects of temper in us are often seen where there are no great flaws of any other kind — and they do more damage to our Christian name than we think. And yet we often treat them as if they were of very small account. We say of some exhibition of hasty anger, or some aggravating word, "Oh! it was only my hot temper, I meant nothing serious by it." Do we sufficiently realise that almost every one of the actings of Christian love detailed in the 13th chapter of 1st Corinthians has to do with the *feelings and the temper,* rather than with the active *life?* How do we make distinctions of blameworthiness where God makes none? Dishonesty, falsehood, impurity, we do condemn, and are ashamed of them; but irritability of temper, proneness to take offence, overweening self-esteem, ungenerous suspicion of motives, evil thinking, and evil surmising — why do we account these not positive sins but only slight blemishes, or even constitutional tendencies that we cannot help?

We do need to have our harsh judgments of others corrected as well as our flattering judgments of ourselves; and nowhere can this correcting of them be effected but in the quiet secret place where we are alone with God, and ask of Him the all-seeing One, to give us the seeing eye that will make our judgments of others more like what His judgment is, and our feelings towards our brethren more like what His feelings of compassionate and merciful love are to us all.

"How blessed, from the bonds of sin
   And earthly fetters free,
In singleness of heart and aim
   Thy servant. Lord, to be!

The hardest toil to undertake
　　With joy, at Thy command,
The meanest office to receive
　　With meekness at Thy hand!

Thus may I serve Thee, gracious Lord,
　　Thus ever Thine alone;
My soul and body given to Thee,
　　The purchase Thou hast won!
Through evil or through good report
　　Still keeping by Thy side;
And by my life, or by my death,
　　Let Christ be magnified!

- Hymns from the Land of Luther.

XX - We Know the Joy of Perfect Self-surrender When We Get Alone with God

ONE of the special joys of the secret hour with God is that then, in still-ness of soul, we can renew our full surrender of ourselves and of all that con-cerns us into the loving hands of Him who alone can "keep us from falling," and " sanctify us wholly," and " make all things work together for our good."

Our self-surrender to the Lord is not a thing to be made once for all at the beginning of the Christian life. It needs to be renewed perpetually: and if it is a duty to make this daily self-surrender, it is also a joy. It wonderfully calms the spirit that has been ruffled by the worries of the day, by the trials to faith and patience that have been met with every hour, and by conscious defeats in the battle with sin, to bring all these disturbing and chafing vexations and lay them down at God's feet and leave them there.

It also wonderfully helps us, when the day begins, and before facing the world again, to have a quiet hour in which to brace ourselves for meeting whatever the day may bring; and then to go forth into its duties and its trials, its temptations and its opportunities, fortified by a strength and wisdom far exceeding any of our own, gained by fellowship with Him.

It is comparatively easy to feel the need of putting our *earthly* concerns into His wiser hands: it is comparatively easy, too, to feel the need of Divine strength for the *great duties* that lie to our own hands: but something more than that, and more difficult than that, is needed too; to put the *soul itself* into His hands, that all its emotions, ambitions, and desires may be thoroughly controlled by Him at every moment of the day.

It is easy to say and feel, "My *times* are in Thy hand"; but we need also to put our *spirits* into His hand for a completer sanctification of what is within, and to do this before the assaults sure to be made upon our spirits have begun: for the spirit is the most vulnerable point of us, and, contrary to what is usually the case in human assaults, none of the outworks fall until the citadel has fallen first. To be securely fortified against such a defeat, " the peace of God which passeth understanding must keep the heart and the mind by Christ Jesus," and to gain that fortifying peace is the blessed work and privilege of the quiet hour alone with God, where we learn to put on the armour that will make us conquerors in the evil day.

For no dependence can be placed on our own power to guard our spirits from defeat. "Except the Lord keep the city the watchman waketh in vain." But what if the watchman be *not* awake, but asleep, knowing nothing till he finds the city taken by the foe? That is a double disaster, and our souls, therefore, must be in better keeping than our own from hour to hour. We need to "commit the keeping of our souls to Him." The power of a Divine Hand must be upon us, the shielding of a Divine Hand must be around us if we are to be, even for one moment, safe. The very same grace that was needed to carry the martyrs triumphant through the flames is needed to carry any one of us unpolluted through the world. The one victory is as truly a Divine victory as the other, and only a Divine Hand can give it. At the outset of the Christian life we know the *saving* power of Christ upon us; in all the after-course of the Christian life we must know the *keeping* power of Christ within us. First we are Divinely conquered; thenceforward, to the very end, we must be Divinely controlled. But this can be a real experience to us only if that Divine control is prayed for and surrendered to in secret every day.

Do not most of us make a great practical mistake as to the way in which our lives are to be brought into subjection to Christ? Paul, writing to the Thessalonians, said, "I pray God your whole spirit and soul and body be preserved blameless unto the coming of our Lord Jesus Christ." He puts the *spirit* first, the *body* last. We often misquote his words as if they ran " your body, soul, and spirit ": but that is not his order, it is the very reverse of it. The first thing we are to look to is the attitude of the spirit, the first thing we are to seek is the rectification of the spirit, and then the other constituents of the whole nature will be sanctified as the result of that. The spirit controls the soul, and the soul controls the body; but if we begin by trying to put the body right before we have yielded the spirit to an absolute Divine control, before we have got that which is the highest force within us put right and kept right, there will be nothing but disappointment and miserable failure in our attempts to subdue the body to God.

That order of procedure will not do. We must begin each day by first of all surrendering the spirit completely to Jesus Christ, our Master and our King; and this enthronement of Christ within us will carry with it necessarily, if it be a real thing, the dethronement of self, the ambitions of self, the plans of self, the will of self, the lustings of self. Full surrender to Him implies His full mastery over us; and till that is both acknowledged as a thing that ought to be, and experienced as a thing that is, there can be nothing in us of that joy and freedom and power that come pouring into the really consecrated heart.

What joy it gives, and strength too, to begin each day by feeling, "On this day once again I am to live simply as a "servant of Jesus Christ: His will and not my own will is to sway me every hour!" "A servant of Jesus Christ!" then I dare not be the servant of sin; I must be holy as my Master is holy. " A servant of Jesus Christ! " then I will not be the servant of men: the maxims of the world will not rule me; I will not take my cue from the world; I am under orders only to my Master in heaven. "A servant of Jesus Christ!" then I *must* be the servant of men, to help them, to comfort them, and to stoop to the lowest offices in their behalf as my Master did. "A servant of Jesus Christ!" then, if His servant anywhere, I must be His servant everywhere; in all society with men I must never forget my servanthood to Him: I must show myself His servant openly as well as confess it secretly. "A servant of Jesus Christ!" then, if I want to know Him, I have simply to imitate Him, to walk as He walked, to plant my feet in His footprints. As the eyes of servants look unto the hand of their masters, to see how their work should be done, and copy what they see, so my eyes "must wait upon the Lord." If His service is sometimes difficult I must not complain: He may use me as He wills. And at the end of all I will be more than satisfied if I only hear Him say, "Well done, good and faithful servant, enter thou into the joy of thy Lord."

To be a true and faithful servant such as this I must put myself daily, by fresh surrender, into Almighty hands, and so I use the words of ancient trust, "Into Thy hands I commit my spirit" for this day and every day till I need them no more. These words Jesus Himself used when, on the Cross, He was looking out on death; but they had been, before that, the words of one who was looking out, not on death, but on the difficulties and trials of life. If they were enough for my Master to die upon they are more than enough for me to live upon, and so I say —

Into Thy *protecting* hands I commit my spirit, for the *keeping* of it. Life is full of temptations, the world full of snares; I cannot keep myself, but Thou canst keep me from falling; I trust myself to Thee.

Into Thy *tender* hands I commit my spirit for the *comforting* of it. The sorrows of my life may be many, the waters deep, the furnace hot; I may have thick darkness over me soon in which I will lose all my joy, but if Thou wilt whisper to me then, "I am with thee still," I will fear no evil.

Into Thy *correcting* hands I commit my spirit for the *sanctifying* of it. I am willing to be chastened if only the chastening makes me purer than before. Take what way Thou wilt with me, I will bless the hand that smites.

Into Thy *moulding* hands I commit my spirit for the *consecrating* of it. Use me for Thy glory. I would not live to myself. Let self be killed that Christ may be all in me. Turn me as the clay is turned in the potter's hands. I would fain be a vessel for the Master's use, filled with the Master's grace, and Thou canst make me so.

Then if death should come even suddenly and call for me, I will hear *Thee* calling, and reply, "Into Thy *redeeming* hands I commit my spirit for the *glorifying* of it. Thy creating hands fashioned me, Thy preserving hands have kept me. Thy guiding hands have led me. Thy appealing hands have beckoned to me, Thy smiting hands have chastened me, but they were always saving hands that delivered me, and sheltering hands that covered me. I ever found them to be loving hands, I have proved them to be strong, and so I trust myself entirely and for ever to Thee; 'Into Thy hands I commit my spirit, for Thou hast redeemed me, O Lord God of truth.'"